CULTURE OF THE FEW

"The Culture of the Few is a great guide for any leader seeking to produce world changing disciples today. In nearly sixty years of ministry, I have never witnessed a group of believers trained as those discipled by Brad McKoy using the principles and methods expressed in this book."

Jim Erb, Overseer, Antioch International Ministries

"This is an important book. Brad shows us once again that history is changed, not by mass-marketing appeals, the most famous, or necessarily the best-organized. History is changed by bands of the brave and courageous few. Brad lives this in real life. His writing comes not from theory, but from true stories that will challenge and inspire you. My prayer is for the Culture of the Few to instill this defining ethic in the body of Christ in the 21st Century and beyond."

Erik Fish, Author and Mission Strategist

"If you only knew what I know, you would be just as excited about the release of Culture of the Few as I am! For over a decade now, I have been privileged to share an exciting missional journey with Brad McKoy. Biblical community actually lived out in the trenches of real-world engagement! Brad goes to Jesus first when asking HOW to pursue mission – then, he just keeps going back to Jesus! AMAZING! This following Jesus obsession is the Kingdom matrix from which Culture of the Few is born."

Dr. Guy Glass, Lead Pastor, Cornerstone Church

"In his typical 'un-churchy' language, Brad has written this book with the heart of a father and the insight of a wise prophet. Knowing how Brad lives his life and this message, I have been anxiously awaiting my copy…and he knocked it out of the park! With engaging stories, humor, and revelation, Brad gives any "would-be world-changers" a path to follow. This is not a book of theories, but truths from the heart of a world-changer with the stories and scars to prove it. "

Jim Baker, Author of [3]How Heaven Invades Your Finances
Senior Leader - Zion Christian Fellowship, Powell, OH

"There are many authors in the world, but I believe it's extremely rare to find people who became their message before they ever preached it. Brad is one of those extremely rare people. I'm one of the many whose life has been changed by the message long before it was a book. This book is a MAJOR resource for anyone looking to introduce the world to Jesus in a long-lasting, sustainable way."

Jasmine Tate, Singer/Songwriter and
Director/Visionary of Artisans

"There's a bandwidth of breakthrough experienced when you come across material that flows from reality, not simply theory. Brad McKoy has lived the message contained in these pages for years. This is an ancient-future book that reclaims the simplicity of living out the gospel and propels a generation forward in the relational advancement of the Kingdom of God."

Brian Orme, Author of Jumpstart and
Little Beans and a Big God, www.iborme.com

"*The Culture of the Few* takes us back to the familiar stories of Jesus for entirely new perspectives. The simplicity and insight in this book has really encouraged me to rethink what it means to change the world and has influenced my approach to family, spirituality and especially - work - in exciting and unprecedented ways. "

Carl Catedral, Co-Founder Adjacency
Entrepreneur /Business Owner

"When I first encountered Brad McKoy I was captivated by his authentic and passionate love of Jesus and community. Over the years I have watched him live out a very clear mission of raising up spiritual sons and daughters and releasing them to change the world. "*Culture of the Few*" is a beautiful description of what I've witnessed in Brad's life. It's not about a program or a prescribed process, but rather it is about knowing Jesus intimately and living that out in each of our relationship journeys. It is then that we begin to see the truth of Brad's words when he writes, "There is a lot of power in a few people living with a focused mission."

Jesse Pratt, Lead Pastor, SLW Church Network

CULTURE
OF THE
FEW

FOLLOWING JESUS.
TRANSFORMING CULTURE.

BRAD MCKOY

 CULTURE OF THE FEW

Culture of the Few

Published by Culture of the Few LLC
121 Grant Street
Grove City, Pennsylvania 16127 U.S.A.

With a mission of developing resources that reinforce relationships,
Culture of the Few LLC is the resource company of author, Brad McKoy.

With a passion to serve people and facilitate strategic paradigm shifts, Culture of the Few author, Brad McKoy is joining with a team of contributors to introduce a new resource platform with the initial content slated for release in the summer of 2016. These resources are being developed to engage leaders with a combination of articles, videos and podcasts that are designed to work together.

Visit us online at www.cultureofthefew.com.

Culture of the Few

LCCN 2016905628
ISBN 978-0-9973976-1-1

First Edition Published by Culture of the Few LLC
Print Book Edition 2016, ISBN: 978-0-9973976-1-1

The Team: Adriane McKoy, Alexander Catedral, Carl Catedral, Candise Wade, Derek Kelly, David Wade, Jessie Woodard, Mike Weber, Michael Giffone, Cody Weber, Katy Westra
Cover Design: Micah List and Stephanie McCloskey Designs
Photography Credit: Alexander Catedral

Printed in the United States of America
First Edition 2016

To those who want to change the world,

This book is written in memory of
Donna Bishop and Lee Myers.

These two, relatively unknown heroes showed me that
you don't have to be famous to make a big difference.
Living with a "YES" in their hearts, they followed Jesus
courageously becoming carriers of the seed of Christ.
The way they lived and died is still pointing people to
LIFE and LOVE.

"unless a grain of wheat falls into the earth and dies,
it remains alone; but if it dies, it bears much fruit."
- John 12:24 (ESV)

contents

foreword

Five years ago, Brad McKoy, walked into our house for the first time. Even though he was a stranger we were just meeting, there was something familiar about him. Shortly after introductions and topical conversation, our two year old son started having a tantrum. He threw the toy he didn't want right in my face and yelled "No!". I excused myself from the room while my husband, Josh tried to keep the conversation going. After a few minutes, they turned to watch the fit escalate. "Excuse me for a minute Brad," Josh said as he walked over to our son. He picked up the little whirlwind of flailing limbs, risking a kick in the face, and took little Jack into the back room to put him in his playpen, saying very firmly, 'No fits." He walked out of the room, and left our son to sort out his feelings about being quarantined in timeout as a discipline for his fit. I searched Brad's face to see his response to the awkward interruption. Would he be annoyed at the dramatic disturbance? Would he look down on us for having a son who had these kind of outbursts? Would he judge the way we disciplined our boy and misinterpret our pursuit to train Jack's little heart to learn patience, self control and honor?

But when I looked at Brad, he smiled. His smile was full of a father's joy. His eyes sparkled. "That was the most powerful display of love right there. You communicated so much by how you handled that little scene. You're a good dad, man," Brad lovingly explained. Since Josh and I didn't know Brad very well yet, we were shocked to hear his words. He brought something into our house that day. It was the kind of conversation you would have with a close friend, a mentor or a family member. Brad cultivates an environment of community around him and carries something unique: safety. We had a platinum record for selling a million albums in a band called Flyleaf and other accolades most people bring up immediately, but he never mentioned those things. He seemed to be more interested in how we loved our family than anything else. I have tears in my eyes as I think of how few people there seem to be who care about that priority like we do. He genuinely cared about our family. Why? As our relationship grew, we realized something about Brad: he carries the Father heart of God.

Brad invited us to come out to Grove City to meet the community of people he works with and disciples at AOX. In every conversation we had with them, we could see that each person had a clear understanding of their identity as sons and daughters. This type of confidence doesn't happen overnight. Most of us carry a lot of baggage we need to get rid of before we can see ourselves as God sees us. I believe this happens through close, consistent relationship. As I looked into each of their eyes, I could see the time that Brad had poured into each of them- making sure they felt heard and understood, but no longer allowing them to believe lies about themselves.

In this book, Brad talks about what it means to cultivate spiritual family. He talks about what it means to know who you really are as a child of God. He talks about how the transforming power of the Love of God flowing through us to others is the way the world gets changed. But what's important for you to know as a reader, is that Brad doesn't just talk about beautiful ideas. He lives them out.

His love is transparent, selfless, consistent, intentional, and beautiful. I'm not saying this to point out how great Brad is, although he is pretty great; I am pointing it out because this is what the heart of God is like towards His creation. Towards His children. Towards His son, Brad. And you can't help believe in Jesus, when you encounter the genuine love of His followers. It is miraculous. Brad's intentional, focused, loving pursuit of the few that God has given him to be family with doesn't just transform the lives of those he touches directly. This love shifts the atmosphere of the coffee shop where spiritual family is simply living life together. Somehow, this love coming from the coffee shop pours out into the street and begins to fill the city. You can feel it when you see the 'Welcome To Grove City' sign.

The love of the Father for his sons and daughters will change everything. But Brad isn't trying to change a city. He is just loving his Heavenly Father back. That love manifests Christ's love to and through others. Relationships that come from this kind of love have consequence. The consequence is changed lives and a changed city. Love and community like Brad talks about in this book will ripple change through generations. It is the Kingdom on earth as it is in heaven.

-Lacey Sturm, Author of The Reason, How I discovered a life worth living

introduction

preface

Several years ago, I had been invited to speak to the Residence Life staff at a Christian college in our town. I was honored by the invitation and had been praying for several days about what to share. As I woke up that morning, I kept hearing over and over the phrase, "Remember the importance of the culture of the few."

That morning, I was aware that while I had never really thought about the phrase "the culture of the few," I knew exactly what it meant. In just a few hours, I was to address twelve resident directors who had been charged with providing a healthy academic, social, and spiritual atmosphere for 2,500 students.

How could twelve people effectively steward the atmosphere of an entire college campus? How could they bring a calm perspective that would help students prioritize and manage their time in a high pressure, academically rigorous environment? And how could this team of twelve do all of this without burning themselves out?

These were the questions I asked myself as I prayed in the shower that morning. My heart got excited as the talk, *Culture of the Few*, began to take shape. Little did I know that years later it would still be shaping me.

1

the power of the focused few

In 2002, my wife, Adriane, and I moved from Wilmington, NC to a small town in Western Pennsylvania to begin the process of planting churches for the unchurched. Our house in North Carolina was just a few miles from the beach, and the fact that we moved away from the warm and sunny south to come to the grey "frozen tundra" of Ellwood City posed a mystery to many of our new neighbors.

"Why on earth would you leave there to come here?"

We had a short list of answers depending on who asked. Sometimes we said how we loved the idea of experiencing all four seasons. Other times we talked about how Adriane didn't like the crazy traffic of the growing city. And then there were those we told that we had moved because we felt like Jesus had invited us to.

There is another answer to the question about our relocation that is relevant to the story. When someone would ask me why I was willing to leave my home three miles from the ocean for the Pennsylvania winters, I would tell them, "To get away from the Hurricanes."

In the few years prior to our move, Wilmington had been a favorite destination for hurricanes and tropical storms. I *still* remember the direct hit we took in 1984 from Hurricane Diana. Over the years, we had several other close calls, which would send my family into "hurricane party mode."

We would clean out the fridge of any desirable goodies, stay up late playing games by battery-powered lanterns, and get a few days off from school. From what I remember, South East North Carolina was spared from any real storm damage for twelve years. That all changed in 1996, however, when Hurricanes Bertha and Fran made their way to our region. They destroyed hundreds of homes and businesses, causing millions of dollars of damage to my city. Hurricane Bonnie did the same in 1998, followed by Hurricane Floyd a year later.

T-shirts were made that read, "Welcome to Wilmington, NC - Choice of 4 out of 5 Hurricanes." One local ice cream stand sold special shakes labeled "Bertha," "Fran," and "Category 5."

So while I didn't *really* leave my beloved hometown to get away from the storms, I was glad they were no longer a part of my life... Or so I thought.

By the summer of 2004, we were getting settled into our new life in Pennsylvania. Following the invitation to "be and do church for people who wouldn't go to church" meant relearning how to do "ministry." We had planted a small "simple church"[1] made up of a committed core of 12 - 15 people and a growing number of new believers. We had started a "missions and relief agency" hoping that it would provide us with opportunities to show God's love to people who were going through a hard time. We fed the hungry, prayed for the sick and hurting, and helped struggling families with utility bills. That fall, the remnants of two tropical hurricanes gave us an opportunity to do even more.

---

1   A good working definition for "simple church" would be a group of at least two or three people committed to following Jesus together.

In all the storms I had experienced in North Carolina, I had seen the damage from a distance, in a way that had never directly hit home for me.

Wow. Things were different now.

Flooding from the storms impacted over 300 local families, destroying dozens of homes in the process. Hundreds of our neighbors were temporarily displaced, and there was no set system to help them.

Prayerfully, I began calling pastors and leaders from the area to see if there was any way that our little "simple church" could help. The pastor of one of the largest Evangelical churches in the region invited me to a community meeting to help assess the total damage and put together a plan of action.

I remember the feeling that I had walking into that meeting. "God, what are these families going to do?"

Once inside, my pastor friend quizzed those in attendance about the extent of the damage in our corner of the county. Tears flowed as community residents described losing everything, many without a clue of where to go next. Some families had been sleeping in tents and cars, while others exhausted their life savings at local hotels. We had to do something to help them.

As the leader of a church of fifteen people, I felt helpless to make any real contribution, but was determined, along with the rest of our team, to do whatever we could. After all, we had moved twelve hours away from the beach to come to this place and show these people how much God loved them. Surely He had a way to meet their needs.

My pastor friend and I helped to form the Northeast Beaver County Flood Assistance Team (NBCFAT). The team consisted of members from several different local churches, and each congregation had a job to do. Our little tribe helped make up an assessment form to determine the specific needs of the families affected by the flood. We spent days and weeks walking the flooded out areas, talking to neighbors, crying with them, praying with them. Once we had the forms filled out, we worked with other members of the team to provide care for the families.

As the weeks turned into months, fewer volunteers were available to help coordinate relief. We ended up with a handful of committed volunteers from around the community, mainly members of my pastor friend's large church and our small one. All of us were astonished at how God provided for people; tens of thousands of dollars worth of resources flowed through the NBCFAT! Drywall, furnaces, clothing and in some cases, new homes were given to help those in need. We even got to throw the affected families a party at the nicest restaurant in our area during Christmastime.

As we served refreshments, gave the kids presents, and provided gift cards to help parents have something to show for the holidays that year, my pastor friend pulled me aside to talk. What he said that night changed my life forever.

Marveling at all the activity in the room, he turned to me and said, "You know, it's really amazing how much the Lord can do through a few people who live life intentionally."

He went on to talk about the impact that our "little church" had made on a big situation.

"You guys have been able to provide more service and man hours than churches twenty times your size. There is a lot of power in a few people living with a focused mission."

While I was honored by what my friend was saying, these were more than just nice words; these were words that changed my grid for success. Here was the pastor of one of the largest, most well-respected churches in the region—a church that had given generously and had been integral in helping hundreds of families—talking to me about the "powerful impact" that fifteen people could make. That if it wasn't for our team going to fill out surveys with the families, the resources that their church had to offer would have had no place to flow.

Something changed in my heart that day. It was not that I had been trying to build a church that looked like his—I wasn't—but I guess in some ways, I still thought that in order to be significant and successful, I needed to reach "critical mass." I thought that bigger, by definition, was always better, stronger and more important, that is until I witnessed first-hand the impact that a small group of dedicated Christ followers could have on the world around them.

That day, my heart started learning to value the culture of the few.

2

so you want to change the world

the culture of the few

What could God do with a few people committed to live a focused life in the midst of the crowd? Throughout the course of history, a simple truth rings out to me: The direction of the masses is typically shaped by the relative few. Influence in the hands of a handful can change the course of history, for better or for worse.

I remember hearing the story of how thirteen people gathered around a young leader near the turn of the twentieth century to discuss a new idea. They believed that within fifty years their "new idea" would rule the world, and in fact, over twenty countries came to subscribe to their beliefs at the height of its popularity, with several major world players still professing it today.

The idea was communism. Thirteen people committed themselves to an ideology that revolutionized the world.

In the introduction of Malcolm Gladwell's book *The Tipping Point*, a story is told of how Hushpuppy shoes were on the verge of extinction until a handful of trend setting students in an artsy neighborhood of New York City decided that the shoes were "cool." Within three years of these students' influential decision to start wearing Hushpuppies, the

brand was stronger than ever before and won the prize for best acces-
sory at the Council of Fashion Designers awards dinner at the Lincoln
Center.

Scripture records the story of how four young refugees rose to
power in one of history's greatest empires. Daniel and his three friends
were literally pulled from amongst the exiled Jews and forced into posi-
tions as princes in Nebuchadnezzar's reign of terror, but they then used
that influence to make decisions that spared thousands of lives.

Culture of the Few is unashamedly written for those who want to
change the world. In many ways this is a book about cultural transformation, and how cultural transformation usually begins away from the
public eye and the flashbulbs of press conferences. Real transformation
is most often catalyzed by a few "agents of change" that live intentionally
and infect others with their lives.

This catalysis is perhaps easiest to see in pop culture with fashion,
art and music. Have you ever thought about the process of "alternative"
music becoming a part of mainstream culture? What was once considered to be "on the fringe" somehow works it's way into acceptance as
the fringe infects the crowd. It starts when someone decides they are
not satisfied with the status quo and recruits a few friends to see things
differently.

These types of decisions don't just shape musical trends or define
what is "fashion forward" for the season; they help determine what
social causes will gain traction and what products will succeed during
the Christmas rush. Politics, family, and faith are all drastically
impacted by those who consider themselves to be outsiders, or different
from the crowd.

Of course, many "outsiders" simply feel discontent and disenfranchised. Negativity and injustice can become both the fuel and the focus of their attention. For some, the discontentment will grow to a place where they are determined to disrupt the norm, forcing change on the masses against their will. While able to make an immediate impact, this kind of lifestyle rarely leads to positive, long-term change.

But there is another type of "outsider" that operates from a different ideology. They are fueled by their quest for justice instead of dwelling on injustice, focusing on solutions instead of problems. Regardless of whether their cause is hugging trees, fighting bad music, or loving lonely hearts, the actions of these agents of change are driven by an intentional desire to see things change.

While there are plenty of outsiders who are content to complain and accuse, these would-be world-changers are not satisfied with empty debates. They will not leave well enough alone. They "scorn the good and strain for the best."

The concept of the culture of the few relies heavily upon the truth that these agents of change have great influence on their surroundings. We can easily forget the impact that the "micro" has on the "macro" if we make the mistake of believing that the masses drive culture. The macro parts of our culture are, after all, made up of multiple micros converging into something larger.

When we forget this important truth, we begin to shift our thinking into neutral, forgetting that we can actually effect change in our own lives and in the lives of people around us. This can be true for governments, businesses, churches and any other social system comprised of people. While the opinions of the masses are not unimportant, they are not typically formed by each member of society coming to the same conclusion both simultaneously and independent of one another. The opposite is actually true.

The crowd is filled with followers. Throughout history, leaders have used this truth to advance humanity towards its greater self or reduce it to its basest qualities. Some have used it to manipulate people into fighting unjust wars. Others have used it to deliver oppressed people from bondage. Despite the positives and negatives of our tendency as a species to "follow the crowd," one thing is certain—it does not cause cultural transformation.

No, transformation occurs when someone makes a bold move that sets them apart from the crowd, a move that says, "Follow me or oppose me, but I'm going this way. I'm wearing Hushpuppies. I won't bow down."

It is easy to think that in order to be an agent of change you must become some revolutionary political leader, but that isn't the case; world-changers are all around us. They are young and old, male and female, black and white. Some have grown their influence to a place of fame and power, but it almost always starts out on a smaller scale.

Yes, if you truly want to change the world you must make the courageous choice to be different. These choices are often made before you ascend to some sort of platform, while you're still in the midst of the crowd. Although this process can be vulnerable, it is necessary for every agent of change. It is in the stepping away from the crowd that you distinguish yourself as someone worth following.

my first encounter with a world-changer

Donna Bishop was one of the first agents of change that I ever had a chance to know. We met when I was a junior in high school. She was a transfer student I had never seen before, but it didn't take long to realize that she was different. I'd often run into this beautiful young woman alone somewhere on campus, just praying and worshipping Jesus. We shared a couple classes and became friends, but she never ceased to amaze me with how serious she was about following Jesus.

Donna actually seemed like a character in a sappy Christian movie. I don't mean that in a bad way, but she said and did things that "normal people" just don't. She had an uncommon heart for intercession, often praying alone in the gym during her free time. I remember her telling me once about her "hit list"—her top ten friends that she was praying to see come to Jesus. She was the real deal, Donna was. So it didn't surprise me when I heard that she was going to become a missionary.

We lost touch after high school, but I reconnected with Donna when I became an assistant pastor at the church she attended. It was a relatively small church that was reaching out to marines who were stationed about forty-five minutes away. Donna and a few of her friends had started hosting Bible studies on Saturday evenings, and some of the marines would gladly use the excuse to get away from base and enjoy a few home cooked meals over the weekend.

One Saturday evening, her little group of friends headed to go get burgers after Bible study when the car that Donna was in got hit. While she seemed to be okay at the scene of the accident, Donna had several serious internal injuries. She was taken to the hospital later that night, and would spend the rest of her short life surrounded by friends and a small but committed army of intercessors.

I was out of town when the accident happened, but I got a phone call telling me that I should come home as soon as possible. I arrived at the hospital Sunday night to find the hallways, waiting room, and chapel all filled with family and friends. Prayer went on around the clock for the next several days as we waited to see what would happen.

I remember walking out into the hallway one evening to find five or six marines standing quietly outside of the doors that led back to the intensive care unit. I was astounded by the fact that most of them had tears in their eyes. I was even more astounded when I found out that only one or two of these men actually knew Donna. Most of them had only heard stories about her from her boyfriend or other people.

In that moment, my mind raced back to my last conversation with Donna, just a few weeks before the accident. It was one of those times when she said things that "normal people" don't say. I had walked in on one of her prayer times and we started talking. She had been praying and meditating on Philippians 1:20-21. Her prayer sounded something like, "Jesus, be glorified in me, whether by life or death. For me to live is Christ, to die is gain."

She hadn't been praying this as a morbid death wish; on the contrary, she was excited to live and become a missionary. Her heart was filled with dreams of friendship, love and family, but her First Love was Jesus and she had given herself to Him in a way that made me a little uncomfortable. She talked about Jesus in such real terms, and lived her life in such a clear way, that it somehow made sense to me that strong men who had never met her were standing in the middle of a hospital with tears in their eyes at the thought of her condition.

That Wednesday afternoon, we all cried when Donna passed away, but we had no idea how God was about to use such tragic circumstances to answer her Philippians 1 prayer. Over the next several months, dozens of people gave their lives to Jesus as people encountered the God that was so real to Donna. Every one of the friends on her "hit list" became believers within just a few months.

Our "little church" was transformed. Over the next three years, over three hundred and fifty people gave their lives to Jesus, including scores of members of the United States Marine Corp. Within six months of Donna's death, we had Bible studies happening on aircraft carriers in the Mediterranean Sea, in Okinawa, and across marine bases and air stations around the United States. The gospel was spreading, and Jesus was receiving glory from across the face of the earth, in part because of one nineteen year old girl who decided to pray and follow Jesus with a handful of friends.

Focus on the Family would later recognize Donna as one of their "Young Women of the Year" in Brio magazine, and our church dedicated a youth center in her honor where we shared the gospel with area teenagers every week for the next several years. As our church continued to grow, so too the number of people who had never personally met Donna increased. Her life had released an influence that still affected them. In fact, the influence of her radical love still affects people to this day.

But the greatest reward that Donna received was not the honors from well-known organizations, or buildings that bear her name. It comes from the answer to her prayer that she would glorify God, be it in life or in death.

multiplying seed

Several years after Donna had passed away, a group of friends, most of whom she had never met, gathered on Saturday nights to hang out at the youth center. Afterwards they would go pray for their friends in the church sanctuary. I didn't always make it to the youth center on Saturdays, but I remember being there one week when my friend, Al, was praying for his roommate, Jeremy. Al and Jeremy were both big, tall Marines, but right about there is where their similarities ended. Al was following Jesus, while Jeremy was a member of a pagan church.

As I watched Al and our friends pray for Jeremy that night, I was reminded of the dozens of people who had come to Jesus in our little church since Donna passed away. I joined in praying for this man that I had never met. There was great faith and expectation in my heart that night, waiting to see what God would do to bring Jeremy to His Son.

The next morning seemed to be a pretty typical Sunday at our church. I was halfway through the lesson I had prepared for the adult Sunday School class when the back door of the church opened. Everyone turned around in time to see a tall marine walk in wearing dark sunglasses and a long, black trench coat. Jeremy had come to show his roommate that his pagan faith would not be shaken by a visit to church.

Jeremy came in and sat down on the second row for the rest of class. He kept his seat as the worship band filed in and our morning worship service began. I remember watching his face as praise filled the atmosphere. At first, his expression looked hard as a rock, but minute-by-minute I watched him struggle to keep his composure as the reality of God's love and presence became real to him. Jeremy didn't make it through the worship service before he was ready to give his life to Jesus.

I will never forget the tears that flowed from the eyes of the now former pagan as we went through the story of the gospel. Jeremy found faith in Jesus that morning, and we baptized him the following week. The change in his life was quite dramatic. I noticed it in measures as he began to grow over the next few months, but it was not until several years later that I discovered just how impactful Jeremy's witness was.

Lee was a staff sergeant that had grown up in the church but had drifted away from Jesus as he entered into adulthood and the marine corp. He was assigned to the same squadron as Al and Jeremy. One of Lee's responsibilities was to check the rooms of the men in his squadron. He was so struck by the change in the atmosphere of Jeremy's room and the change in the content of his locker that it brought him under conviction. He started hanging out with another friend who had recently started following Jesus, and it wasn't long before Lee had rededicated his life to the Lord.

One man (Lee) had recommitted to following Jesus because of change in another man's (Jeremy) locker, who had started following Jesus in part because of his roommate's (Al) prayers, a roommate who had come to Jesus as a result of the gospel going out from a youth center named after a girl (Donna) whose life seemed to end too soon.

During the seven years I had the privilege of serving as one of the pastors of that "little church" in North Carolina, my life was forever altered. One of the things that changed me the most was the truth God taught me from the events surrounding Donna's life and death: You don't have to be famous to change the world and eternity.

I left North Carolina in 2003, but I continue to see how the lives Donna touched are still making a difference. Most of those young marines have grown up to be husbands and fathers leading families that love Jesus. Their children have probably never heard the whole story about how a nineteen-year-old girl gave her life to Jesus through prayer and intercession. They may not know the story, but they have become a part of it.

"Jesus, be glorified in me, whether by life or death. For me to live is Christ, to die is gain."

dear would-be world-changers...

If we are going to follow Jesus, the idea of being a "world-changer" should be as natural as the sun rising in the East. The desire to effect change is a good thing, and for a disciple of Jesus, it is a part of the invitation to "Come, Follow me." And that is ultimately what this book is about.

God is not looking for the next Billy Graham or Mother Theresa. He is not in heaven wringing His hands hoping that someone will step to the forefront and write a book like CS Lewis used to write. The world is not waiting on the next great conference speaker, nor is it longing for some edgy church planter to move into a warehouse and start a trendy new community of faith.

The world is waiting for you.

In fact, all of creation waits eagerly for the sons (and daughters) of God to know who they are and simply be themselves.

It is easy to imagine traveling to third world countries or speaking to the masses and think, "That would really make a difference." There is nothing wrong with those things, but if we hold on to this Christian fantasy of becoming something special for Jesus, we allow our identity to flow out of "what we do" instead of "who we are." The greatest thing you can do to change the world is to follow Jesus and to be who God made you to be.

I'd like to submit that you can do more for Jesus by encountering His love everyday and overflowing onto those around you than you ever could with a stage and a microphone. Those things aren't bad, but if you simply draw close to Jesus each day and allow the power of the Good News to transform your own "status quo," you will become that catalytic agent of change in the process, impacting eternity in ways you never could have imagined or checked off on a list. That's because God is love, and once we realize we are made new in His image, we become free to both receive and be His love to those around us.

Remember Donna's story. It is exceptional in many ways, but in no way is it the exception. History is filled with stories of influential movements that were sparked by lives that went seemingly unnoticed on this earth. Remember that a life that has been given to Jesus becomes seed in the hands of the Father. It is His job to work transformation through us, as we yield ourselves to Him and live out our lives in holy confidence, a confidence that comes when we are free to be who He made us to be.

I was only twenty years old when Donna died, but I have been blessed to spend a majority of my life following Jesus with other passionate, young "world-changers". My friend, Lee Myers, (who you will hear more about later) was one of these leaders. One night, he invited me to come to Allegheny College and speak to a few dozen students from around the region. As I stood to begin, I remember looking up and realizing the magnitude of the collective destiny in the room that night. Tears began to fill my eyes as I tried to speak. Although it doesn't happen often, that night I was speechless.

After several quiet minutes, I opened my mouth and asked, "What do you say to a room full of people who will change the world?" I felt the desire of these young leaders to know and encounter Jesus putting a demand on my heart that night. There were things stirring in me that I didn't know how to explain. The hunger for Jesus in that room was both astounding and humbling. These people were not following Jesus so they could have a nice life; they were convinced that following Jesus would change everything in them and that they, in turn, would change the world.

following the ultimate agent of change

If we were to look back through all of history's examples, no one modeled the truth of the culture of the few more clearly than Jesus. While His public ministry was filled with stories of healing the crowds, He spent most of that time focusing on twelve ordinary men. He especially poured into three; three years, focusing on three men, who would be integral in forming and leading the church after His death and resurrection.

So yes, it is true that Jesus spoke to the masses and fed the thousands, but He spent His life focusing on the few.

Many times in Scripture we find Jesus performing miracles and giving parables to the crowds, but there was always something deeper for the few back at the house. To the crowds He would say, "He who has ears, let him hear..." but to his disciples He would reveal the meaning of the message, saying, "To you the Kingdom has been given..."

Jesus knew that the crowds were susceptible to the spirit of the day. They cried out "Hosanna" one week and "Crucify" the next. It was not the chanting thousands that waited for the promise of the Father in the upper room ten days after His ascension, but the relative few.

What was so different about this son of a carpenter from Nazareth that prompted Him to invest in a handful of fishermen from Galilee instead of allowing the masses to make Him king? He was free from the expectations of how greatness should be measured in the eyes of man. Resisting the religious and political opportunities of the day, Jesus chose instead to draw greatness out of common, unschooled men and to be identified as a friend of sinners.

What can we learn from the life of Jesus in regards to transforming culture? He sees men responsible for "turning the world upside down" inside a group of ragtag disciples. The rest of this book will be dedicated to discovering what it was that allowed Him to give Himself to these men with full confidence that it was God's best plan to change the world. We will journey together to find out what made Jesus the ultimate "agent of change," and we might be surprised at how different it looks from our expectations.

SECTION I
identity

3

destiny flows from identity

Jesus was, without a doubt, the ultimate agent of change. His life was so transformative that all of history hinges on His incarnation. What happened Before Christ had to be distinguished from everything that happened After Christ.

It seems somewhat ironic to me that we can spend a lifetime trying to follow "Jesus the belief system" without ever allowing the way He actually lived to influence our lives. We will spend a large majority of this book examining the life of Jesus with the intention of following in His footsteps today.

The remainder of this book is divided into five sections, each dedicated to a different core truth that I believe are keys to living out the culture of the few. Each section will consist of several chapters. This first section will focus on the issue of identity in the life of Jesus. We will primarily examine how Jesus understanding His identity was crucial to living out the culture of the few. With this in mind, we will study two key stories that provide insight into exactly *how* Jesus understood His identity.

setting the stage

As we go back two thousand years to the time when Jesus walked the earth, let us remember the setting. Palestine, along with most of the rest of the known world, was under the control of the powerful Roman Empire. The Jewish people, God's chosen people, had been eagerly awaiting the arrival of the coming Messiah. This "Anointed One" would deliver God's people from their oppressors.

From time to time, some hopeful prospect would catch the eye of the public, leaving Israel wondering if Messiah was about to reveal himself. I can easily imagine a group of "Messiah Watchers" that acted as the expert panel of their day, who had a grasp on all of the prophetic promises about the coming deliverer. They would have been able to present an image of Messiah that left every Israelite ready for that deliverer to come with might and destroy the yoke of Roman tyranny.

Each religious sect lobbying for influence within the Jewish Sanhedrin undoubtedly projected a preview of the Promised One that served its own views. We know that others arose in the years leading up to the days of Jesus claiming the title Messiah, but none ever lasted or proved to be truly Him. This only increased the Israelites' longing for the true Promised One's appearance.

Word began to spread about a strange man who was attracting crowds, baptizing hundreds in the Jordan River for repentance from sins. Some called him Elijah; others thought him a prophet. But could this weird, country preacher be *Him*?

There was a man sent from God, whose name was John. This man came for a witness, to bear witness of the Light, that all through him might believe. He was not that Light, but was sent to bear witness of that Light.[2]

John preached a simple message: "Make straight the way of the Lord." People get ready. He was known for his strange diet and wardrobe, but what really set him apart was the fact that he welcomed people down into the Jordan River to be baptized. He said that he baptized people in water as an act of repentance, but there was Someone else coming who was greater. One who would baptize with fire and the Holy Spirit.

These claims must have seemed fantastic to those gathered on the riverbanks hearing him preach. Some must have wondered, "Just who does this guy think he is?" while still others put their hope in his word. Yet day after day, John went on about the promise of the coming of "One greater than I." [3]

Then one day, John looks up and makes an announcement to his flock: "Behold, the Lamb of God!" Imagine the gasp that went up over the crowd as every head turned to get a look at Messiah. What would the "Lamb of God" look like? Who was it? While I cannot gossay for sure, I can only imagine their sense of disappointment and skepticism when the crowd realized that John was pointing to... his cousin. I can just hear the scoffers scoffing: "I knew this guy was a phony. Let's get out of here before they take up an offering..."

But then Jesus does something that surprises everyone. Even John. Especially John. Jesus, the 'Lamb of God', insists on being baptized—in the Jordan—by his redneck cousin. This is not what the people of Israel had been expecting.

This was not the mighty warrior king rushing to their rescue. He was not decked out in armor and riding on a white stallion. He was wearing carpenter's clothes and walking into a dirty river to be baptized with the same baptism that was being offered as an act of repentance to sinners.

---

3   Luke 3:16

Nevertheless, Jesus continued on into the waters. With each step He made a statement. To some, that statement disqualified Him as a legitimate candidate for Messiah. "There is no way that we have been waiting all these years for this." But in reality, Jesus's actions crushed the fantasy of what Messiah "should" be in order to reveal the very nature of God.

I can imagine the "experts" conferring with one another to find out if there was any possible way that this humble carpenter from Nazareth could really be the Messiah. The Scriptures certainly do not describe a scene that would look like a national political convention, but I like to imagine that Jesus saw the pundits huddling together, criticizing His every move. Whether or not the "Messiah Watchers" were there on that day, we do not know. But we do know that He continued down into the waters.

Jesus was free to step into the Jordan because He wasn't concerned with the expectations of man. He knew the truth about who He was, and that it was who He was that mattered. It didn't matter if He met all the expectations of what people thought He should be. It didn't even matter if the crowds accepted Him or rejected Him. Before He set one foot into the water, Jesus already knew what God was about to announce to the rest of the world: He was God's Son.

understanding the source of significance

Some eighteen years earlier, when Jesus was just a boy, he had gone on a trip with his parents to Jerusalem. Several days into their journey home, Mary and Joseph realized that Jesus was not with the rest of His relatives as they had thought, and so headed back to Jerusalem to find Him. Can you imagine the terror that was going through Mary's mind?

"I've lost the Messiah... How could this happen? I am the worst mother ever..."

For three days they search in all the places that you would expect to find a twelve-year-old Messiah. I can imagine them searching through camel stalls and soccer games and dreidel shops, only to be both amazed and relieved when they end up finding young Jesus at the temple, sitting at the feet of the teachers. He was listening to them and asking questions that revealed such an uncommon understanding of the Scriptures that it left onlookers astonished.

Can you imagine the parental exasperation in Mary and Joseph's hearts as they found Him there?

Jesus Christ Emmanuel the Lord, where have you been? Why did you do this to us? We have been worried sick looking all over for you!

"Why were you looking for me? Didn't you know I would be looking after My Father's business?" [4]

I have heard the story of Jesus as a boy in the temple my whole life. (I still remember what the flannelgraph images look like from Sunday school.) Yet only recently have I begun to understand the true significance of the story. This is more than a snapshot glimpse of adolescent Jesus. This is not just filler for the life story of Messiah. There is an important message for us to see here.

At the end of their search, Mary and Joseph find their boy, and He is genuinely surprised that they did not know where to look. It was only logical to Jesus that He would be in the Temple, busy about His Father's business.

---

4   Luke 2:41-52

Long before the Father ever spoke words of affirmation at His baptism, Jesus knew who He was. Throughout His whole life, He had the issue of His identity settled in His heart. He was His Father's Son.

destiny flows from identity

Jesus lived His whole life aware of His Father's love. That love was His identity, and it wasn't subject to change based on His actions or other people's opinions. I believe that is why He was free to step into the baptismal line and identify Himself with sinners. He already knew who He was.

Time after time throughout His life, Jesus seems to make choices that set Him apart as a champion of the sinful and socially impoverished of His day. This was important, because He said that these were the ones He had come for, those who were lost. Whether it was dining with tax collectors or allowing harlots to touch Him, Jesus did not allow the fact that others were scrutinizing Him to determine what His behavior should be. Jesus never allowed opinion to hinder love.

Jesus grasped the truth that His significance upon the earth did not come from the approval of any man, or even from the resumé' of His righteous deeds. His significance came from His Father. Jesus models that when we understand that our identity flows from sonship, we are free from the need to measure up to the expectations of man and the pressures of this world. That is why "identity" is the first of the five foundational truths for living out the culture of the few.

When our hearts can truly grasp the significance of belonging to the Father, it will free us to live life from a different perspective. At the same time, when the issue of identity is left unsettled in our hearts, both our motives for wanting to impact the world and our definition of success will be skewed.

As those who were created in the image of God, we were created with a sense of significance. When we are able to clearly see that this significance comes from our Father, we can worship Him and steward who He made us to be out of a place of purity; but when we think that significance is something to be earned or attained, it can lead us to a broken way of living life. Our quest for significance can actually fuel a pressure to perform that can lead us away from the Father.

In the next chapter, we will look at how we can follow Jesus in embracing a life of sonship. We will explore how living with a healthy understanding of our identity can shape our lives as agents of change.

4

my name tag says son

As we begin to look at how we can follow Jesus into a greater under-standing of what it means to be a child of God, it is important that we do so through the lens of the culture of the few. Why is understanding our identity so important? How does it relate to cultural transformation?

These are good questions and they need to be answered. Understanding where our true significance comes from is essential because it will free us from living under the pressures of needing to mea-sure up to the broken rulers of this world. It is hard to see real cultural transformation take place around us when we still long for affirmation from the culture we are trying to transform.

Living with a clear understanding of our identity allows us to approach life with nothing to prove. We become free to love, serve and invest into culture around us with no strings attached. This is the way that Jesus lived, loved and led. Because he did not need to be affirmed by the world, He did not need to be conformed to its standards. This is important, because when we try to conform ourselves to society, we lose the ability to transform it.

Jesus did not enter into His earthly ministry in search of signifi-cance. In fact, as we look at His life, I believe we will see that it was His confidence in His identity as a Son that released Him into the impact of the last three years of His life. Why do so many of us have this backwards?

It can be easy to spend our lives striving to become somebody for God and continuously falling short. Plagued by our own humanity, sin and shortcomings, we face constant inner turmoil as we try desperately to make a name for ourselves. A distorted pressure to "change the world for Jesus" or have "our own ministry" can weigh us down, leaving us unsatisfied with life.

I believe that many young "would-be world-changers" struggle with this everyday. While it is normal to have a heart to make a difference, we cannot allow the pressure to "become somebody" rob us of the joy that comes from recognizing the significance of who we already are.

The life of Jesus reveals the freedom and confidence that flow from belonging to the Father. Simply put, Jesus fully embraced His sonship here on the earth. Defying any need to "become somebody," He allowed the Father to determine the priorities of His daily life by only saying what He heard the Father say and doing what He saw the Father do. Instead of trying to make a name for Himself, Jesus was satisfied to be known as His Father's son.

Yes, I am aware that Jesus was God and we are not, but that fact was not meant to become an obstacle. Jesus meant it to be an invitation. He left the glory of heaven and became God incarnated in the flesh on this earth so that we could become like Him. He humbled Himself as a man so that He could walk as an example of what it meant to bring heaven to this earth by living in communion with His Father.

Communion with the Father was what drove the life and ministry of Jesus. More than the mission that He was sent here to accomplish,

Jesus desired to do the will of the Father on the earth. The more we practice following Jesus in embracing this life as a son or daughter of God, the freer we will be to bring heaven to earth out of our relationship with the Father.

measuring up

One of the biggest challenges world-changers face is the sense of weight or pressure that rests on their lives. Between the burdens and passions of our hearts, and the prophetic words that we carry, we can walk through this life feeling overwhelmed by all that we need to accomplish. But have you ever thought what it must have been like to be Jesus for the first thirty years of His life?

This was the Son of God—the One present at the creation of the world—and He lived in obscurity as the son of a carpenter for the majority of his time on earth. He was aware of His royal pedigree, but the people of Nazareth probably drew their own conclusions about the "miraculous" circumstances that surrounded His birth. But Jesus knew why He had come.

His mission to redeem the world would have been enough to weigh a normal man down. And prophetic words? There were hundreds of prophecies that pointed to what His life would be:

Redeemer.
Savior.
Lamb of God.
Emmanuel.
The Christ.
Wonderful Counselor.

Mighty God.

Everlasting Father.

These titles and names were impressive, each carrying a certain weight that demanded respect. Yet of all of the names that had been prophetically attached to the life of Jesus throughout the Old Testament, why did He choose "son" as the name by which He would be known?

Jesus is referred to as either the "Son of Man" or the "Son of God" over 130 times in the New Testament, and this is also the primary way He identifies Himself.

"…just as the Son of Man did not come to be served, but to serve, and to give His life as a ransom for many." [5]

Yes, Jesus came as the Messiah, the Christ, and the Promised One—but He chose to reveal Himself as a son. And by doing that, the veil was lifted. What was eternally true about God was now revealed to all of mankind. He is Father.

This revelation of sonship is what turned the religious world upside down. For centuries, God had been known as Creator, King, Judge and Ruler of All. But Father? Very rarely was that imagery used in the Old Testament. Then Jesus splits eternity, and the Firstborn Son was born to become a first fruit of many others to follow.

the process of Sonship

Although Jesus came as Son to restore us to the Father as sons and daughters, His sonship was important for another reason. Jesus modeled how to live and relate to the Father as a son in this world. While it is

---

5   Mark 10:45

true that Jesus had the advantage of being completely sinless, Scripture also make it clear that in becoming a man, He subjected Himself to every temptation that we encounter.

The manhood of Jesus is something to be celebrated because it was central to heaven's plan for redemption and restoration. Jesus came to this earth fully God and fully human, but Paul tells us in Philippians that while He existed in the form of God, He emptied Himself to assume the likeness of men—to become like us—and set aside his divine rights to take the form of a servant. By His humility in obedience to the Father, Jesus made Himself into an example that we could follow. This ultimate act of sonship provides a clear picture of how we can move past knowing that we are God's children in our theology to actually becoming sons and daughters of God at a cellular level.

There is a process that living out of our identity will lead us into. Often time it is humbling and draws us into some seemingly hidden places. Jesus experienced this at a carpenter's shop in Nazareth. Yet there is something so powerful about the hidden life of Jesus, something that speaks so strongly to what it takes to live out the culture of the few: He was born a King, the Christ, Messiah, and yet He was relatively silent for thirty years.

During that time, there were no miracles or public ministry to speak of. No sermons on the mount or clearing out of temples. How could this be? All of eternity was waiting on the arrival of the Christ, but then He arrived and seemed in no hurry at all to save the world.

It is not as if the birth of Jesus went unnoticed. There were angels, shepherds and traveling wise men. King Herod was so terrified by the birth of the King of the Jews that he ordered the execution of thousands of baby boys. While it is true that the identity of the Messiah was not revealed to the masses at the nativity, the events surrounding the birth of Jesus shook the world.

I can imagine that the shepherds who were present on the hillside around Bethlehem that night must have wondered what happened to that baby in a manger. For years they had told the story of the how the host of angels had appeared to them, lighting up the dark night sky. They had waited to see what would become of the Savior whose birth had been announced to them. I wonder how many years it took for them to begin to question if anything would become of the little Christ child.

Jesus just did not seem to be in a hurry to enter into His public ministry. All we really know was that He knew He was His Father's son at twelve and that He had worked as a carpenter from Nazareth. Thirty years. His Father's son. A simple carpenter.

I do not want to read between the lines too much and try to draw something out of a story that is not there. Scripture remains largely silent on the matter. I do, however, want to point out something about Jesus' public ministry that I believe He picked up long before He turned water into wine. Central to the message that Jesus preached as He traveled from town to town, and imperative to the miracles that He performed to demonstrate that message, was that He knew how to wait on the Father.

In becoming one of us, Jesus took on the limitations of our humanity. While remaining fully God, He lovingly humbled Himself to be restrained and confined to being fashioned as a man. This is such a powerful part of the ministry of Jesus. He did not rely on His understanding of the doctrine of healing to bring wholeness to those around Him. He operated out of knowing what the Father was doing and understanding that His role was to bring the will of the Father to earth. This is what allowed Jesus to live His life tucked away in the carpenter's shop for thirty years.

It is not that His heart was not moved with compassion when He saw the blind and the lame during those first thirty years, but that He was willing to wait until His Father said it was time for Him to move out from the carpenter's shop. When Jesus intervened on behalf of the woman caught in adultery, was that the first time He had witnessed a mob seeking to take judgment into its own hands? What must it have been like for Him to remain silent, waiting for the release from the Father to announce to the world that He had come to fulfill the law that no one else could keep?

Jesus practiced a restraint over the course of His public ministry that should cause us to reevaluate our view of ministry. For instance, everyone that came to Jesus with a physical need was healed, but there are stories recorded in Scripture where Jesus did not heal everyone present. John chapter five records the story of Jesus healing the man at the pool of Bethesda. Jesus walks into a room full of needs and sees a certain man that had been sick for thirty-eight years. John does not record Jesus speaking to anyone except him. Out of the estimated hundreds of sick people present, Jesus recognized that the Father was highlighting one certain man.

I believe that a part of the process of sonship Jesus modeled for us was His willingness to be restrained by love. By submitting Himself to do only what He saw the Father doing, Jesus passed up many good ministry opportunities. He did not claim the royal rights at age eight like King Josiah, but instead waited patiently and faithfully for His Father to say that He was ready.

By doing this, Jesus trusted that the love of the Father for Him was more than enough to satisfy every one of His needs. He also trusted that the Father's love for the world was sufficient to lead Him as He walked this earth, and that God would release Him at the time He would have the most significant impact. Because He embraced sonship, Jesus knew that whether He was feeding the five thousand or cutting logs into boards, that as long as He did what He saw the Father doing, He was bringing the Kingdom of God on earth as it is in heaven.

so send i you

Grasping the goodness of the Sonship of Jesus sets us up to walk with Him as sons and daughters. For those of us who hear the call to "come and follow" Him, this is vitally important. I believe sending Jesus as a son was central to heaven's plan for redemption.

Every time that Jesus places an emphasis on His relationship with God as Father in Scripture, He is also emphasizing sonship. When Jesus speaks to His friends in John 20, it is as the risen Son that He addresses them. While Matthew 28:20 is commonly known as the Great Commission, John 20:21-22 also contains a powerful, apostolic assignment:

> So Jesus said to them again, "Peace to you! As the Father has sent Me, I also send you." And when He had said this, He breathed on them, and said to them, "Receive the Holy Spirit.⁶

Jesus came as a son, and I believe that He emphasized the Father in this passage to remind His friends that they were also being sent out as sons. Only a few days earlier, He had told the twelve that He was sending the Holy Spirit so that they would not walk as orphans in this world. Now He is sending them out to make disciples of the nations and releasing the Spirit of sonship to them as He does.

---

6   John 20:20-21

Paul says in Romans 8 that all of creation is waiting and groaning for the revelation of the sons (and daughters) of God. I find it interesting that Paul did not say that creation was waiting for apostles, prophets, evangelists, pastors and teachers. No—the world is waiting, with baited breath, for the children of God to manifest their true identity as they more deeply know and understand the boundless love of the Father towards them as His sons and daughters.

Jesus modeled this life for us and released His followers to live out of that same paradigm. Understanding the importance of *Identity* is not only important to living out the values of *Culture of the Few*, it is foundational. Everything else must be built on top of knowing who we are as sons and daughters of God.

One of the most radical ways that we can follow Jesus is by embracing sonship. We will spend the rest of this chapter looking at how Jesus *actually* restored our relationship to the Father and how that should effect our mindset on what it means to become children of God—two important truths that can help us practically follow Jesus into reshaping our identities.

come to Papa

The first of these truths is that Jesus came to restore us into a real relationship with the Father. This is more than theology; it is an invitation to know God as our Dad. When Jesus walked the earth referring to Himself as a son, He was tampering with the image of who Israel understood God to be. The terminology used in the New Testament to describe God as Father is most often "Abba". This would not be translated today as "father" in a formal sense, but as "papa" or "daddy".

Even though I am part of a church culture that places a high value on intimacy and practicing the presence of God, this "papa" approach can seem uncomfortable and too familiar to my understanding. But in the life of Jesus, the God of Isaiah 6—the One who is "high and lifted up", and whose train "fills the temple"—chose to reveal Himself as Abba.

Make no mistake about it: He is still "Holy, Holy, Holy," but through Jesus the "Son" we find that He is also "Daddy".

Can you imagine how angry the Pharisees and the other religious leaders of the day must have been when Jesus showed up and proclaimed *I and the Father are one?* If it is still uncomfortable for many of us today, what must it have been like for those who heard the very words come from Jesus' lips?

By proclaiming that He was the "Son of God", Jesus redefined God as "Father" and insinuated that it was "Father God" that had sent Him to come. This is important; for it was as a son that Jesus became the Way, the Truth and the Life that we might come to...the Father.

When I was a child, I had a friend from school that lived on an exclusive island off the coast of North Carolina. I had heard about Figure Eight Island for as long as I could remember. It was where movie stars and politicians lived. Well, one day, my friend invited me to come spend the night.

When the day of the sleepover finally came, my parents picked us up from school and we headed off to his house. I was so excited to get to go spend the night. No longer would this special place be a figment of my imagination; I was going to stay there for the weekend! But as we drove up the road to the bridge that led to his house, I encountered a problem: a tall, locked gate stood between the island and me.

The guard inside the gatehouse had the job of making sure that only those who could prove that they belonged on the island could cross the bridge. Somehow, I thought we'd be in trouble.

Our vehicle didn't have the special sticker that all of the other cars in line with us had. I felt nervous. Would we be allowed to cross the bridge and get onto the island? My dad rolled his window down as the guard asked if he could help us. Then my friend chirped up from the back seat.

Hey, it's me. This is my friend Brad and he is staying the night with me.

Just like that, the guard smiled and raised the gate. We were instantly granted access to cross the bridge because we were with someone who belonged. The guard recognized my friend, and I was allowed onto the island because I was coming home with a son.

I must admit that for most of my life I thought that "Father", "Son" and "Holy Spirit" were more the "job titles" of God than anything else. That being the Son was a job that someone had to do to take care of our sins. In John 14:6 I thought Jesus was saying, "I am the Way, the Truth and the Life, no man comes to salvation except through me." But that is not what Jesus said. He said you cannot come to My Father unless you come with me. We gain access to the Father because we come to Him with His only begotten Son. The One He loves perfectly became a man so that all of creation could be reconciled to His Dad.

The goal of the gospel itself goes beyond the salvation of our souls from sin and hell. The goal of the gospel is that through the life, death and resurrection of the Son, we who were once far away are brought close and restored to the Father. That we who were orphans find a place at the Father's table.

Being 'the son' was more than a job title; it was the essence of who Jesus was. It is true that there were hundreds of prophecies about what Messiah would be like, but when Jesus showed up, He didn't rely on His prophetic words to tell Him who He was. The prophetic words relied on His identity as God's son.

Jesus came as a son so that He could grant access to us to become sons and daughters with Him. He became the firstborn son, so that He might be first among many brothers. He entered this world in humility as a human so that we might become more than mere servants of God like the angels are. The angels long to look into the salvation of the redeemed, blood bought sons and daughters of God. Simply stated, Jesus came to us so that we could come home to Father.

The incredible cost that Jesus paid at the cross to restore us from our sin into a relationship with God was worth it in heaven's plans. We have been transferred from the kingdom of darkness into the Kingdom of the Son of His love. This is more than a theoretical, theological position. It is an invitation to embrace the eternal life of knowing the Father by following the Son. As we follow Jesus, let us make sure to make room in our lives to follow Him in being intentional about coming to the Father through the life of the Son.

becoming sons

We can come to the Father because of what Jesus did on the cross, but it can still be challenging to believe that we *really* belong in His presence. It is easy to accept that I have access to God because of Jesus, but the thought of actually living life as a son or daughter of God is a stretch. For the rest of this chapter, we will focus on the importance on what it looks like to become sons and daughters of God.

But as many as received Him, to them He gave the right to become children of God, to those who believe in His name: who were born, not of blood, nor of the will of the flesh, nor of the will of man, but of God.[7]

When I talk about *becoming* sons, I am focusing on the transformation of the way we think about the fact that we have been adopted into God's family. Again, this is more than a mental assent that we have been born again and are children of God in a generic sense. *Becoming sons* means that I am no longer destined to live life as an orphan under the bondage of fear. I am free to embrace what it means to belong to a Father who has chosen me to belong to Him.

I have a friend who has been blessed in many ways, including financially. He and his wife have a heart for orphans and adopted several siblings. Things went very well with his adopted daughter, but his adopted son struggled with the transition. For most of his life he had been an orphan.

Did you know that there is a significant difference between the way that orphans and sons approach life? Orphans don't have the luxury of receiving hugs and kisses and "I love you's" from a mother and father. They may not know where they will live next month, or even if there will be three square meals the next day. For my friend's son, he struggled to build any kind of real attachment to his new family. Instead of being able to enjoy the blessings of his father's house, he related to the world out of his experience as an orphan. He could not grasp the love of his new parents or the benefits that came with being their son.

Many believers have been duped into thinking that while we may be the children of God from a doctrinal vantage point, that in this life, we are still orphans. Failing to grasp the goodness of our Dad, we grovel as spiritually pitiful paupers instead of walking out our role as princes in

---

7   John 1:12

our Papa's Kingdom. The saddest part of this may be that a counterfeit understanding of the Scriptures have allowed so many to embrace this theology as truth, lessening the power of the message of the cross. If it had been God's plan to redeem us up to servant status, that would have been better than hell and more than we deserved, but it was His good pleasure to restore us to the place of His very own.

I believe that there is a process of becoming a son in our thinking. It is sometimes painful to face up to our orphan fears and welcome the Father to replace those fears with His love, but it is worth it. It is important to invite the Holy Spirit—the one that Jesus promised would come so that we don't have to live like orphans—to help us understand what it means to live life as sons.

Growing in this area of thinking like sons is really the key to having our identity settled in Him. Though at times it feels like a spiritual fiction to believe that I am *holy and blameless before Him in love*, choosing to believe the truth of our Father's words over our lives will bring freedom to receive the perfect love that He has always had for us. In the next chapter, I will share a bit of my own journey to embracing sonship.

8   Ephesians 1:4

5

living with an unfair advantage

my own story

Things had gone from bad to worse. I remember lying across my bed feeling like such a complete failure. Our ministry was falling apart. Our income was gone. Relationships that I had thought were lifelong covenant friendships had dissolved. The lone bright spot in this bleak season had been the arrival of our precious little girl, Abigail.

For the first time in my life I recognized that I was struggling with depression. Gone was the excitement about our growing church plant. The calls for me to come and preach at churches around our region had stopped. No more radio interviews or newspaper stories. Friends seemed distant. I felt exposed as a failure, ashamed of the outcome of my ministry.

My thoughts of self-pity were mingled together with an apologetic prayer: *Lord, I sure am sorry for the mess that I seem to have made down here. I was only trying to obey You, trying to love people and lead them to You. I feel like I have failed in every area: as a husband and father, as a ministry leader, as a son. I am sorry to bother you with all of this...*

As I lay there crying, my thoughts went back to when I was a little boy. While I have always loved and adored my mom, my dad has always been my hero. I looked like his mini-me, right down to the same haircut and style of glasses. We loved doing things together. We would play ball, wrestle, and go fishing. Every once in a while, my dad would even reward me by allowing me to miss a day of school and going to work with him.

I remember the feeling of significance that came from being the only eight-year-old insurance salesman in my class. I would dress up in my little shirt and tie and be off to work with Dad. It was so exciting to be out of school and in the car on our way to our first appointment. The excitement would last for about the first ten minutes of my dad's presentation and then...

What could a rambunctious eight-year-old with ADD do for 45 minutes while my dad explained Medicare to senior citizens?

I tried to remember all of the things Dad had told me. Sit still. Don't break anything. Please try not to interrupt me. And most of all: DO NOT PICK YOUR NOSE. I don't know how successful I was at following my father's instructions, but he always made me feel like his partner and continued to allow me to go to work with him. Even though selling Medicare supplements was not something that particularly interested me, I loved being with my dad, and over the course of time, I memorized his presentation.

One day we stopped by my dad's office before heading out for our first appointment. When I walked in, everybody made a big fuss. "Oh, wow, Tom, he looks just like you..." I will never forget turning around to see the look on my dad's face. He was beaming with pride. Then he looked at me and said, "Son, why don't you go ahead and explain Medicare to them?"

The small sales team gathered around as I went through and diagramed Parts A & B of Medicare on my dad's yellow legal pad. "Wow, not only does he look just like you, but he sounds just like you too." Still brimming with pride, my dad reached out and put his arm around me and said, "Yes, that's my boy."

Through the memories I began to hear God the Father speak to me in a way that changed my life.

"What qualifications did you have as an eight-year-old to be an insurance salesman? What did you bring to the table that would help your dad sell insurance?"

A picture of me sitting there on one of my dad's clients' couches trying not to pick my nose popped into my head. I began to realize that my dad didn't ask me to work with him because he needed my help, but because he loved me and he loved having me with him.

I thought back to that moment in the office and heard the Father say, "Brad, I love you and I love it when people see the ways that you look like Me. I am proud of you and proud of the way that I made you. And when you take the time to listen to what I am saying, I love it when others hear My voice in your words. I didn't call you because I need you or your giftings, but because I love you and it gives Me great joy that you care about My business."

Immediately, the weight of my failure began to lessen. The pressure that I had been carrying to be successful in ministry so I could make something of myself was gone. In that moment, my heart caught the fact that my significance did not come because I was an eight-year-old insurance salesman, but because I was my father's son.

living with an unfair advantage

I was born with an advantage. In fact, I've had an unfair advantage my whole life. It is an advantage that cannot be bought or earned. It is the advantage of sonship[9]. From my earliest memories, I have always known that I was a beloved son. I have a mom and dad who have loved me every day of my life. As a child, I would wake up to find my parents weeping and praying over our family, lifting my sisters and me up to the Lord.

I have known my parents' affection and deep love from the very beginning. They have celebrated me not only on my good days, but even on my worst. I can honestly say that I cannot remember pillowing my head once in my life feeling that I was outside of my parents' love and favor.

I knew that I was loved because my parents told me they loved me. Multiple times each day, I heard an affirmation of their love for me. But it was more than just the words and the accompanying hugs and kisses. It was watching the way they prayed and worked to lead and provide for our family. It was recognizing the look of joy on their faces when I would bring them a picture that I had drawn, and even as a child knowing that the joy did not come from the quality of the drawing but from their love for the artist.

I also knew my parents loved me because of how they corrected me. In fact, I would say that the way my parents approached discipline was probably one of the most important shapers for the cultural development of my heart. My dad spanked me "early and often." It didn't take a Class 3 felony for me to receive the "rod of correction." Their approach was based on consistency to produce godly character in my life. When I was four or five years old we actually had a family project cutting out a paddle for use on my rear end. We used that paddle for the rest of my

9   When I speak of sonship, I am referring to belonging to the Father as a son OR daughter.

spanking career. By the time we were through, there were layers of duct tape around the handle to keep this special family heirloom intact.

I am writing these details for you because they were such an important part of my life. My parents never beat or abused me. They never punished me out of anger, but with a firm love they modeled humility and brokenness. I always understood the reason for my spanking and I always, always knew that I was only being spanked because my parents loved me. It was common for our spankings to end with my dad holding me, and both of us crying. We would pray together that God would help me remember how to do what was right.

My parents "early and often" philosophy was based on the hope that if they could build godly discipline in my sisters and me early, that with God's help, it would produce character in us that as we grew older it would be able to stand against grownup challenges and temptations. Looking back, I am sure that there were times my broken behavior tested their philosophy. But my wrong choices never jeopardized the love that I received from them.

I do remember one time as a teenager, getting caught in an especially bad situation. My sin was exposed, and I was afraid. I remember wondering if I had finally found the eject button that would send me out of my father's love and favor. This situation was a big deal. Big enough that I knew that the events of that day could be a game-changer for the rest of my life. I had done something terrible. I had been caught, guilty of my sin. In my mind at the time, if my parents would have decided that they didn't want me in their home anymore, they would have had just cause. I never questioned their love in those moments. I did question if the greatness of my sin would be more than their love could handle.

I was right, it was a life-changing day for me. When my parents spoke to me that night, they did it firmly and without any compromise to the standards of what it meant to live in their home. There was no room in my mind for me to think that my actions were "not really that big of a deal" or that they were acceptable in any way. But this firm love was spoken over me as they held me and cried with me. At the end of the talk, both of my parents told me that they loved me and that there was nothing that I could ever do that would make them stop loving me. They told me that they were so thankful that God had given me to them and that they were proud to be my parents.

It was official. This was my worst day, and at the end of it I was still a beloved son in my father's house. I don't know how this translates to your heart, but it changed my life forever. It silenced the accusations of the enemy that "if you ever get caught, your parents will never want to see you again." The events of that day testified that what my parents had been telling me all of my life was true. They would love me no matter what.

The rules of life and love in the supposed "real world" are all based on performance. You scratch my back, and I'll scratch yours. What have you done for me lately? I'll love you forever if you (fill in the blank). These are a part of the basic principles of this world that Paul told the Colossians we have died to. We don't have to live by these broken rulers any more. When I say that I live with an unfair advantage, it is the advantage of sonship. It is the advantage of living with the security that I am loved and that I belong. No matter what.

Win, lose, or draw, I know that at the end of the day my mom and dad are going to love me, and that they are proud of me. This knowledge has brought me to a place of real freedom. It has brought me to a place of receiving the Father's love with security. Because I know that His love for me does not rest on my ability to earn His favor, I am free to follow Jesus as a son, not as a slave. I know that I don't need to build a successful ministry to be somebody. I don't need to become a "big success," to make something big out of my life. I am already significant to the Father because I was formed by Him and for His pleasure. He gets excited to hang my "finger paintings" on His refrigerator, not because my artwork is all that great, but because His face lights up when I walk in the room. I am my Father's son.

finding Daddy

"And you shall know the truth, and the truth shall make you free."
- Jesus Christ

The truth of the gospel is not found in grasping an accurate doctrine about man's need for salvation. Knowing the Truth is more than merely understanding correct information. Knowing the Truth is knowing Jesus and the freedom that He came to bring. It means coming to the Father and being made a son in His household. It means finding Daddy and hearing His invitation to abide with you, and for you to make your home in His love.

We cannot progress into the other principles of the culture of the few until we grasp the foundational importance of living out of our identity as sons and daughters of God. We cannot effectively follow Jesus into seeing society transformed until we grasp His perspective on life and ministry.

Sometimes, it is easy for those with world-changer mindsets to try to be a noble servant of God and to disregard the fact that our hearts were made for love. God is not asking you to go through life feeling disconnected from His goodness so He can use you to do something great. Jesus came to earth so you could come to the Father. Because of His sacrifice, you can draw close to the throne of God. The throne of heaven is your Papa's chair. Press into the heart of God for a greater understanding of His unconditional love for you.

All of your desire to impact the world for Jesus will not be enough to sustain you if you don't have love. The conviction of God's calling in your life will not satisfy the deepest need of your heart to be perfectly loved. His love for you is perfect, and His perfect love perfects you, setting your heart free from fear and from abandonment.

I have already shared my own story with you, how in a moment of hurt and despair, my heart was set free from the bondage of needing to become somebody for God, and I realized that I was already somebody to God. I was His son. Shortly after that story, God took things a little further with me.

I was standing in the bedroom of our tiny apartment holding my daughter, Abigail. She was about four months old at the time. She was old enough to recognize me, but not old enough to really communicate. As I was standing there, two things happened that the Father used to demonstrate the reality of His love to me.

First, I recognized the immensity of love that was in my heart for this little girl, as I held her in my arms. So far, she had done nothing but eat, sleep, cry, giggle and make messy diapers, but she had stolen my heart, and I couldn't imagine loving her anymore than I did in that moment.

As I looked down at her, I sensed God speaking to my heart.

Remember that every good and perfect gift comes from me, the Father of lights. The love that you feel towards your daughter right at this moment is just a drop in the ocean of what I feel towards you. My love for you is full of the pleasure and satisfaction that you are feeling towards Abigail.

In that moment, the Father's love took on a more tangible dimension that propelled me farther into understanding His heart. God's love is more than good theology; it is the essence of His person. To know Him more is to know His love for me.

What happened next wrecked my heart even more. As I studied my little girl's face with all the joy of a father, she looked up and gave me the most incredible smile. As her face lit up, I felt so much pleasure in my heart. Pure pleasure unlike any other feeling I had ever known.

Again, I heard the Father speaking to me:

The pleasure that you feel when your daughter looks at you is just a drop in the ocean of what I feel when you look at me. When you turn your attention towards me and give me your full affection, my heart is satisfied. When you worship me and tell me that you love me, it really does bless me, and I receive it as love from you.

As I stood in the middle of the room, weeping and holding Abigail, my heart melted. I had grasped the significance of sonship a few months before, but now I was truly finding the Father's heart for me. I was experiencing His pleasure in a way that I didn't know was possible. Not only was I discovering the depths of God's love for me, but also the King of heaven had made Himself vulnerable to my affections.

The apostle Paul talked to the church at Ephesus about knowing God this way. In the middle of his prayer for the Ephesians recorded at the end of chapter three, Paul prays for the believers to be "rooted and grounded in love," and that they would be able to comprehend with all the saints what is the width and length and depth and height—"to know the love of Christ which passes knowledge; that you may be filled with all the fullness of God."

The Father's heart for you is for you to know a love that goes beyond your ability to understand. The word "know" in this context means "knowledge gained through experience." It is God's plan for you to experience the fullness of His love in this lifetime.

i see me

Understanding our identity helps us begin to grasp the significance of the Father's heart for us. As this happens, it shapes our perspective of life in ways that are hard to imagine. It allows us to clearly see the truth of God's love. It also helps us look past the distortions of the brokenness that the realities of this world present to us.

God really showed me this several years ago, as I was trying to work with our godchildren on Scripture memory. Every Sunday morning, people from our simple church would come over for brunch, and we would spend time together. After brunch was over, I would pick a Bible verse and teach it to Jace and Gloriana. Jace was seven, and Gloriana was a very precocious four-year-old.

My goal in teaching them the verse each week was to go beyond Scripture memory and help them to discover the person behind the words. On this particular Sunday, I was teaching them one of my favorites: Proverbs 16:15. *In the light of the king's face is life, And his favor is like a cloud of the latter rain.* My main objective that week was to teach Jace and Glori the importance of seeking the face of God.

Jace was getting it pretty easily, but Gloriana was struggling a bit. I decided that maybe she would understand things easier if she could act it out, so I sent her about twenty feet down the hallway and asked her to stop and face me.

"Gloriana, look at me," I said. "Now what do you see?"

"Uhh, I see you, Uncle Brad."

"What else do you see?"

She frowned. "I see the sofa you are sitting on, and the window behind you..."

She did not seem too enthusiastic about my object lesson. I had her walk about ten feet closer and then asked her the question again.

"Gloriana, what do you see?"

This time she let out a little huff before she answered. "I see you, Uncle Brad."

"What else do you see?"

"The same things I saw before," she said. "I see the sofa and the window."

"Look closer, Gloriana," I said. "Can you see any thing else?"

I could see her little eyes focusing as she started to notice details that she could not see from her original view. Now we were getting someplace.

My goal was for her to see that if she got closer to me, then she would be able to see me in more details. I had her come and stand right in front of my face. I was sure that this would help her to understand my point. Little did I know that she was getting ready to go beyond that and to teach me one of the most important lessons I have ever learned.

As she stood just a few inches away from my face, I repeated my instructions.

"Gloriana, look at me. Now what do you see?"

As I have already stated, Gloriana was a precocious little four-year-old. As she opened her mouth to answer, I watched her facial expression change from the kind of exasperation a teenager trapped in a four-year-old's body would express at being asked the same question for a third time, into amazement and wonder.

"Gloriana, what do you see?"

"Ah!" she squeaked. "I see me! I see me!"

It took me a moment to figure out what she meant. Then it hit me. Glori was standing close enough to me that she was seeing her own reflection in my eyes. I think my spirit went into shock that morning as God used a child to teach me the lesson of a lifetime.

When we get close enough to God, not only are we changed from glory to glory as we behold His beauty, but we become free to see ourselves in His eyes. When we see ourselves in the eyes of His love, it is without all of the distortions and brokenness of this life.

When we determine to pursue God as a loving Father, with the confidence that we belong in His presence because we are His children, it will free us to get close enough to see ourselves in His eyes. Who you are in the Father's eyes is who you really are. Your experience in this world will try to convince you that you are guilty and condemned, but through His eyes, you are Holy and blameless before Him in love.

Ephesians 2:6 says that you are already "seated with Christ in the heavenly realms." We know that Jesus is seated at the right hand of the Father, which means that we are too. I believe that we were meant to live this life from the lap of our Father, drawing close to His heart, looking deep into His eyes.

Gloriana ended up writing a song that encapsulated our experience a few months later. The lyrics reveal to me that her encounter led her into an important truth.

I know You're here, I know You're true.

I know You're my Father up in heaven.

I know You're God, I know You are my Father,

And I know we are Your sons and daughters.

I have watched the reaction to this song in amazement as it has been sung over congregations, conferences, house churches and other groups of believers. Something takes place in both the old and the young as this simple, foundational truth settles into minds and hearts of those who hear it. It's like I can almost see people's thoughts being rewired as they sing a song written based on a child's encounter with God.

Before you move on into the rest of the content of this book, I want to invite you to stop and meditate on how much the Father loves you.

SECTION II
invitation

6

come and see

Understanding who God made us to be brings so much freedom to our lives. As we move forward in this book and look at the other four foundational truths in *Culture of the Few*, they are all established on the core truth of Identity.

When we understand the significance of our own identity, it releases the Father to reveal it to everyone else. We see this expressed so clearly in the life of Jesus. I believe it was His clear understanding of who He was that allowed Him to move freely into the Jordan River to be baptized.

Following Jesus into this kind of freedom will empower us to walk with the confidence and courage necessary to make world-changing decisions. Confidence and courage, harnessed with humility, freed Jesus to shift the atmosphere of His surroundings at His baptism. In fact, it was what happened immediately after He came up out of the water that had everyone talking.

When He had been baptized, Jesus came up immediately from the water; and behold, the heavens were opened to Him, and He saw the Spirit of God descending like a dove and alighting upon Him. And suddenly a voice came from heaven, saying, "This is My beloved Son, in whom I am well pleased."

Can you imagine what it would have been like to be there? Whether those in attendance were among the disappointed or curious, it is certain that none of them were expecting this baptism to come with special effects. You and I have the advantage of living in a day where 3-Dimensional, computer generated images are commonplace. Our minds have a grid for what this scene could look like if Stephen Spielberg had been hired to direct the movie. But for those who had come out to see a country preacher in the wilderness, in the days before subwoofers and silver screens, this was unlike anything they had ever seen.

The heavens opened to Him. The Holy Spirit, in the form of a dove, descended and rested on Him. And then, the voice of the Father, the One that Israel worshipped, spoke out saying: "This is the One, My beloved Son. My pleasure rests on Him."

I don't know if they had false teeth back in the day, but I can just about see dentures falling out as the whole crowd stood there, jaws dropped in amazement. Any sense of disappointment was gone. Wonder now filled their hearts. This was certainly something to write home about. After thousands of years, the Messiah had come.

The stage was now set. What would Jesus do for an encore? How would Messiah set up His non-profit? Where would His headquarters be? Who would He select to be on His board of directors?

Stewarding the momentum of open heavens, descending doves, and heavenly voices is not for the faint of heart. This was a major moment. It was time to call in the media for a press conference and capitalize on the opportunity for Jesus to establish His own ministry. He could have released a new book, announced the opening of a ministry school, or posted service times for a crusade at the local arena.

Everyone who had heard about His baptism was asking one question. What would Jesus do next?

Again, the next day, John stood with two of his disciples. And looking at Jesus as He walked, he said, "Behold the Lamb of God!"

The two disciples heard him speak, and they followed Jesus. Then Jesus turned, and seeing them following, said to them, "What do you seek?"

They said to Him, "Rabbi" (which is to say, when translated, Teacher), "where are You staying?" He said to them, "Come and see." They came and saw where He was staying, and remained with Him that day.

Evidently, Jesus skipped the after parties that one would have expected to be thrown for the occasion. The next day, we find Him together with His cousin John and two of John's disciples. I believe that what happened in this moment is recorded in Scripture for an important reason: It captures the essence of God revealed through the life of Jesus and reveals the second principle in cultivating the culture of the few. Jesus lived His life with a spirit of invitation.

In the same way that Jesus told the disciples to "come and see," Scripture is full of invitations from God to His people.

Taste and See that I am good. Call me, I will answer you and show you great and mighty things that you can't imagine. Seek me and you will find me.

Hebrews tells us that Jesus is "the brightness of His glory and the express image of His person…" In other words, Jesus is the exact representation of God on the earth. If we look at how often God extends invitations to His people, then we should not be surprised that Jesus, the One who reveals His true nature to us, would do the same.

we've had It backwards

Many years ago I read an article in a magazine. I don't remember learning anything new from the article, but it's content encapsulated what I had been learning in that particular season of life and ministry.

The article explained how throughout the last several centuries of common church culture, we have created an unhealthy matrix that we force people to go through to really become a part of "us"—AKA the Church. The basic concept can be summed up in three words: Believe, Behave, Belong.

The first thing we do is find out what they BELIEVE.

In many churches, the sermon ends with, "If you died today, where would you go?" This question is followed up by a sixty-second presentation about the highlights of the gospel. Sometimes it's from Romans, sometimes from John, but at the end of the sixty seconds, the newcomers are told that if they want to go to heaven, all they have to do is believe these four things in their hearts.

Now pray this prayer, and you're in.

Please don't get me wrong. I believe that we *must* be "born again" as Jesus told Nicodemus. But sometimes we ask people to believe in Someone we haven't introduced them to yet.

So they pass the BELIEVE test, professing faith in Jesus. Then what? Naturally, we want to see how they BEHAVE.

This is the step that causes Protestant churches to have about a bazillion different options for newcomers to Jesus. Not only are we asking them to conform to the way we believe, we then accept them based on whether or not we like the way they act.

What kind of clothes do you wear?

What music do you listen to?

Do you think it is okay to say _____?

Do you watch R-rated movies?

Then we have *another* list of BEHAVE questions for how you act in church.

Do you like to clap your hands?

Do you speak in tongues?

Do you tithe?

Again, it is not that behavior is unimportant, but when we place so much emphasis on the way people act, we put a pressure on them to do just that—act.

So now they believe the way we believe, and behave the way we behave. What's next?

While no one would ever actually say these words, the message that we send to the world rings loud and clear: If you believe the way we believe, and behave the way we behave, maybe one day you will have the chance to actually BELONG here.

This is such a broken way of inviting people to experience God's love and His family. BELONGING is the gospel. That orphans get adopted, that strangers find family, is the core of Christian belief. Not only is Believe, Behave, Belong a broken invitation; it is exactly backwards from the way Jesus did it.

Think back to our Savior, a twinkle in His eyes, as He walks past the two disciples. "Come and see," He says. "Come and see."

belonging

We don't know all the details about what happened next; the Scriptures simply say, "They came and saw where He was staying, and remained with Him that day." (John 1:39a)

Jesus did not stop to quiz them on their theology or ask them what they believed about Him. He extended a simple invitation to them in response to their curiosity. "Where are you staying?" He invited them to come find out and to belong together with Him. Once they came and saw where He was, they remained with Him. As we will talk about in more depth later, Jesus follows the "Come and see" invitation with "Come, follow me."

Jesus knew that for someone to know Him, they needed to encounter Him. He lived His life as an open invitation for people to encounter the heart of God through His life. The crowd listening to Jesus share the story about the prodigal son was filled with "sinners" who were always being drawn to Him because of the spirit of invitation that was on His life. When we are secure in our own identity, it releases a confidence in us to live a life that is accessible to others.

This book is in large part about the power of transforming the culture around you by investing intentionally in a few people. Jesus modeled this as a lifestyle while still living as an invitation to everyone He came in contact with. I am not suggesting that you focus on the few in a way that is connected to small thinking, or neglecting the masses. I believe that Jesus poured intentionally into a few because He knew that it was the best way to disciple the nations.

Jesus had a pretty specific strategy in inviting people to BELONG with Him right from the start. He knew who He was. Confident of the power of the Spirit that He carried, He knew something that we have forgotten in the church today: That if people really belong and remain together with Jesus, it will change the way they BEHAVE.

"I am the vine, you are the branches. He who abides in Me, and I in him, bears much fruit; for without Me you can do nothing."

Jesus is telling His friends that the key to producing Kingdom fruit is abiding or "remaining" in Him; that apart from Him we can do nothing. Could it be that by inviting people to BEHAVE before they BELONG we are inviting them into the frustrations of fruitless living?

Jesus invited "unschooled, ordinary men" to walk with Him, knowing that if they remained with Him their lives would be transformed, that their walks would begin to look more like His. The fact is Jesus began discipling people long before they ever BELIEVED. He started discipling them from that first invitation to come and encounter Him.

It was not until the end of the last supper, after Jesus had told His disciples about His coming death, having stripped down and washed their filthy feet, not until He had loved them to the end, that they really BELIEVED.

"Now we are sure that You know all things, and have no need that anyone should question You. By this we believe that You came forth from God."

Again, I am not underestimating the importance of believing. But even after the disciples had witnessed the miracles of Jesus, even after they had been sent out to heal the sick and drive out demons with their own hands, there was still something unsure and unsettled in their hearts. They walked with Him. They moved in the power He carried. But only after that special supper were they truly able to move to a place of confident belief, and Jesus didn't hold it against them.

Jesus invited people to BELONG knowing that would lead to a change in the way they lived life (BEHAVE). In sharing His life with them, He was leading them into a confident heart BELIEF that came from truly knowing and trusting Him. The disciples had tasted and seen, and it was way too good to pass up.

Why have we been doing things so differently from the way that Jesus modeled life for us? We have separate strategies for evangelism and discipleship. Sometimes, it seems that the people that we "lead to Jesus" end up being a completely different bunch than the ones we release into ministry. Could this flow from the disconnect between how we evangelize and how we disciple?

Jesus engaged people by inviting them to come share life with Him, knowing that *knowing Him* is what would really make the difference. Those who heard the invitation were the people He spent the next three years of His life with. They were the same ones He commissioned to go disciple the nations when His time on earth was completed.

Learning to live life as an invitation is important to living out the culture of the few. Invitation creates access for people who do not follow Jesus to encounter the transformational power of the Good News. It also creates a clear example for new disciples, teaching them that they too can live a life that invites others to encounter God's love. Because we are confident in our identities as recipients of the Father's love, we can cultivate a lifestyle that invites people to experience that love in ways that a lifeless form of religion never could.

We have been focusing on the way that Jesus invited people to walk with Him (discipleship). If we can learn from *how* Jesus called His disciples, what can we learn from the types of people He called?6

7

who Jesus called

Central to the message of this book is the fact that Jesus entrusted His life's work into the hands of ordinary people. The heart of the culture of the few relies on the fact that there is great power in ordinary people being influenced to a place where the status quo becomes interrupted. The influenced become influencers, and their message is multiplied as the ordinary become empowered to share their experiences with others.

This principle applies to all types of social change. We can see it in the way that advertisers rely on the power of word of mouth in their marketing strategies and in the importance of cultivating grassroots networks in political campaigns. As ordinary people become passionate receivers of a message, there is great potential for that message to spread as the receivers are empowered to become carriers of that message. That is why it is important to look at the way that Jesus invited people to follow Him AND to look at the type of people that He called.

Often times, much is made of the diversity of the twelve. I think this is done to show us that Jesus is interested in fishermen and tax collectors, radical religious zealots and those in whom there was no guile. This is true, but if we primarily look at the twelve through the "diversity lens," we can easily miss that most of these men were family and neighbors.

As many as eleven of the twelve apostles were from Galilee, with a number of them being from the same hometown of Bethsaida. Many missiologists believe that the twelve apostles were all between the ages of fifteen and twenty-five. If this is true, then not only were most of these guys from the same neighborhood, but they were also all close in age. If the twelve apostles had lived in twenty-first century America, many of them would have gone to "Lakeside High School for Future Fisherman" together. Some of them would have been in the same graduating class.

It is easy for me to think that when it was time for Messiah to build His ministry team, He would have scoured the land looking for the bravest, brightest and best that Palestine had to offer. I can imagine that it involved an assessment form that included a personality profile as well as a spiritual gift inventory. But that is not the way Jesus went about calling the twelve.

Of course, we do not get a detailed explanation of the hiring strategy, but this is what we do know: The day after Jesus was baptized, Andrew asked Him where He lived. Jesus said, "Come and see." Some time later, presumably after Jesus was led into the wilderness, Jesus approaches Andrew and his brother, Peter, and invited them to "Come, follow me." He went a little farther and finds two more brothers who happen to be Andrew's neighbors. He extends the same invitation to James and John as He had to Andrew and Peter.

We know that Phillip was another fisherman from Andrew's neighborhood. Jesus found him and said, "Follow me." Phillip found Nathaniel and introduced him to Jesus.

Are you seeing the pattern here? Jesus was not conducting interviews with the elite candidates from Apostle Preparatory School. He met Andrew and invited him into the place where He stayed. Then He went and found Andrew in the place where Andrew lived life and invited him to walk with Him. He invited Andrew and his brother. He invited Andrew's neighbors to walk with Him as well. In turn, the neighbors started finding other friends and introducing them to Jesus.

Jesus invited people to know Him and follow Him. It cost them something to do that, but in return He said that those who would lose their own lives would find what life could really be. He both invited people into His life and engaged them where they lived. This is a strategy that will still work today.

the keys are in the pocket...

The way Jesus connected with the twelve was by reaching Andrew and his "pocket of people." The fancy, missiological term for "pocket of people" is *oikos*. The Greek word oikos literally means "household." While sometimes used to talk about a physical structure shared by a family, often it refers to the family (or sphere of influence) itself.

Throughout the life of Jesus, we see Him reaching an individual and subsequently their "pocket of people" get saved or impacted as well. We see this in John 4 with the woman at the well. He encounters her in the midst of her everyday responsibilities and then reaches her whole town because of her testimony. This was also evident when Jesus recognized the hunger of Zacchaeus as he entered into Jericho and called him to come down out of the sycamore tree. He invited Himself to Zacchaeus' house that night and proclaimed that, "Salvation had come to his house (oikos)."

The model of reaching a household was central to the instructions that Jesus gave His disciples as he sent them out in Luke 10. In fact, He tells them that as they enter a city they should find a house (oikos) that they can bless with their Peace, and that they should stay there and focus on that house for as long as they are in the city. I believe that this is what Jesus did in reaching Andrew and his "pocket of people." This oikos became the core of the early church, those who turned the world upside down.

Remember, most of these men were family members and neighbors. They may have had different vocations, but there was a strong common connection between eleven of the twelve. If you are wondering which one of the twelve was not from Galilee, his name was Judas Iscariot. Interesting indeed.

fishing tales

There is one other commonality that we find in many of the twelve. These men were fishermen, either professionally or recreationally. We know that Peter, Andrew, James, John and Phillip are specifically named as "fishermen," but there are stories included in the gospels that indicate that most, if not all of the twelve found themselves out fishing from time to time.

He called them away from the casting of their nets to come fish for men. I know that we could say that Jesus was just putting the invitation of following Him into terms that were relevant to His audience—and that may be true—but I believe He intentionally called fishermen first.

So in focusing on what we can learn from who Jesus called, let's take a look at *what they did*. What exactly were these anglers from Galilee up to when Jesus came and invited them to follow Him?

casting nets

When Jesus came to the first set of brothers, Peter and Andrew, they were fishing. They were casting their nets. This is the fun part of fishing, because it's the part where you actually catch fish, which is, after all, the whole point.

There is a process of catching fish, and it starts with trying to find them. I believe that this part of fishing represents the work that evangelists are to equip us for: the intentional investment of the gospel among people who do not yet know Jesus.

When Jesus extended the invitation for Andrew and Peter to become fishers of men, they would have understood that it would include seeking out men in an active way. After all, Jesus said that He came to seek and to save that which was lost.

Peter and Andrew were men who understood that in order to catch fish, you have to go to where they live. We know from a later story where Peter's mother in law was healed, that he lived in a house, not on a boat. That means that when Peter woke up each morning, he had to make a decision to leave where he was to go to where the fish were. As we grow in becoming fishers of men, we have to do the same thing.

It has never been the job of the fish to come to where we are, but it is all too common in church culture for us to spend a lot of effort in decorating our churches and customizing our gatherings in a way that will attract fish. We can learn so much from Peter and Andrew. They were fishermen who knew that in order to catch fish, you needed to go out and get wet.

Intentionally investing our lives in the places where people who do not know Jesus live and work and play must become natural for us. I find it all too common that well-meaning Christians, who have a heart to follow Jesus, don't have any part of their lives where they are making room to spend time with people who have never met Jesus. But we must remember that following Him means becoming fishers of men.

I have a friend named Erik Fish who has an infectious passion for seeing people come to Jesus. I have learned so much about becoming a fisher of men from him. He has spent much of His life equipping and stirring up the body to reach the lost. I have watched the light bulb go off for seasoned pastors and young college students alike as Erik points out this truth from the first chapter of Mark's gospel: Following Jesus means that He makes us into fishers of men. It was not an optional part of the invitation, but an expected outcome of walking with Him.

I think one of the greatest misconceptions in the church is that making disciples of the lost is only for those with the gift of evangelism, or for the pastor. It is not just for the more extroverted followers, or for those who are comfortable with sharing their faith. Jesus is still seeking and saving "that which is lost," and if we intend to move beyond being a believer and answer His call to become His followers, then we will have to go out there with Him.

Compelled by His love, we must go beyond our all-too-comfortable comfort zones, and rely on the Comforter to help us do what can be so uncomfortable. Every follower of Jesus can see the life-changing message of the gospel transform the lives of people who do not know the One we follow.

the problem with mishandling dynamite

In my journey of following Jesus, I have found that the gospel works. As someone who grew up hearing about Jesus my whole life, I found out that hearing about Him and knowing the stories were not enough for me. I needed to encounter the power of the good news in a way that would transform my life.

In Romans 1:16, Paul says that inside the Good News about Jesus is a power to bring salvation to those who will receive it. The word "power" in this Scripture comes from the Greek word *dunomus*, which is where we get the word for dynamite. There are other times that we see the English word power used in the New Testament that comes from a Greek root meaning "legal authority" or "power of attorney." This is an important distinction.

There is a big difference in a "power of attorney" and a stick of dynamite. Both are useful, but I have found that in my own life I need to encounter more than just the "power of attorney" to change me. I need to come face-to-face with the explosive power of God to transform me into a man who looks more like Jesus.

The thing is, the gospel does work and it changes our lives. It will also change the lives of men and women who have never heard of Jesus. It worked for me; a proud, religious wannabe who was addicted to lust and shackled by shame. I have seen it work for those caught in the clutches of crystal meth, prostitution, and pornography. I have seen the gospel work for social orphans in search of family. I have seen it work for those with broken sexual identities, transforming them into confident, maturing men and women. The gospel works.

The dynamite power of the gospel has the power to displace us from darkness and into the Light. That's what dynamite does. It changes things. It always has and it always will. Regardless of the changes to our culture, the good news about Jesus will always be more than enough to bring humanity to salvation. It will do what it does best and restore orphans to the Father until the King returns. But did you know that the gospel working can actually create problems for us?

If we as the church are not ready to disciple those whose hearts are coming awake to the light of Jesus, we leave these new believers believing that Jesus and the gospel does not work, at least not for them. When we preach the message of the gospel to bring people to a new birth and fail to disciple them, its like going through all of the labor to deliver a precious baby and then leaving it alone in the hospital room to fend for itself.

This often happens when people who have grown up outside of cultural Christianity come to Jesus. They can have a genuine encounter with God and become born again, but outside of a discipling relationship, they are left alone to try to figure out how to follow Jesus on their own. Scripture teaches that none of us were intended to follow Jesus alone. When we ask new believers to do this, we provide them with an inferior encounter of dynamite, and we set them up to fail.

Jesus says, "Come," but that means we go

When Jesus first encountered Andrew, He extended the invitation to come and see where and how He lived, but that next invitation is what would really satisfy Andrew's curiosity to see what the Messiah's life was like. As Jesus spoke the words, "Come, follow me," He was inviting Andrew and the others to go beyond knowing about His life. He was inviting them to share it.

For three years, twelve men went with Jesus wherever He went. They walked the same roads that He walked, ate the same food that He ate, and slept in the same places He slept. As Jesus walked the earth, crowds gathered from town-to-town to see Him, each urging Him to stay with them a little longer; but "the few" knew that He was a "going" Messiah. Even though the crowds insisted, He kept moving.

But He said to them, "Let us go into the next towns, that I may preach there also, because for this purpose I have come forth."

Jesus lived to complete His journey. For the twelve, knowing that "the going" was an important part of following Jesus while He was on earth must have prepared them for the commission that they received before He ascended back to heaven.

"Go therefore and make disciples of all the nations, baptizing them in the name of the Father and of the Son and of the Holy Spirit, teaching them to observe all things that I have commanded you; and lo, I am with you always, even to the end of the age."

This was not the first time that Jesus had sent out His few. He sent the twelve out in Luke 9, and by the beginning of chapter 10 there are "seventy others" who joined them in the going. Jesus was equipping them and sending them out to cast their nets, to find a pocket of people and share the love and power of the gospel of the Kingdom of God there.

That was two thousand years ago. It is tempting for us to think that the call to follow Jesus has changed over time. We hear the "Come to me all who are weary," the "Come and see," and even the "Come, follow me," and somehow forget or miss that coming to Jesus will eventually demand that we go. He is the same yesterday, today and forever. In the twenty-first century, Jesus is still moving. I believe now, more than ever, the gospel is a "going message," going out in power wherever those who are following Him end up.

For Andrew and the other fishermen, they received this great commission knowing that Jesus would soon be leaving them for good. He had told them that His time on the earth was drawing to an end, but that He would soon send His Spirit to be with them. At the end of His instructions to disciple all nations, He made a promise that must have meant so much to these lowly, ordinary men. He said, "I am with you always, even to the end..."

This meant more to them than a flowery closing to a religious speech. These were His friends, and He was committing to be with them, even after He was gone. Andrew had experienced the times when Jesus had made a difference. He was with them in the boat several times, when it seemed they were doomed. In over their heads, with storms raging around them, their lives were spared by the presence of the One who could speak, "Peace, be still."

Jesus had also been with them when it seemed they were wasting their time. Having fished all night with no fish to show for it, they heard Him say, "Cast your nets on the other side." At least twice, Jesus led His fishermen few into a supernatural catch when their best attempts had been fruitless. So a promise that He would stay with them in the midst of His leaving and their going would have meant a lot to Andrew and the others—probably everything. It would have bolstered their spirits with confidence, hope, and courage to keep casting their nets until they had turned the world upside down with the message of the Messiah.

In learning about who Jesus called, we can see that He invited ordinary men to walk with Him. Over the three years that He spent with them, He modeled a lifestyle of fishing for men. He trained them to go find the fish, and left a promise that He would leave His Spirit to be with them even after He was gone.

As we continue to look at the culture of the few, we will look at another part of fishing and how living with a spirit of invitation is important in equipping followers of Jesus to live as fishers of men.

8

the other part of fishing

We have looked at how Andrew and Peter casting their nets is a picture of the evangelistic focus of following Jesus and being fishers of men, but when Jesus went a little further down the sea shore, He found James and John busy doing something else.

When He had gone a little farther from there, He saw James the son of Zebedee, and John his brother, who also were in the boat mending their nets.

If casting nets is the fun part of fishing, then mending nets is the necessary part. I believe this picture demonstrates the importance of shepherding within the body of Christ.

Fishermen are famous for telling their fishing stories, and over the years I have heard my share of "whoppers." I have heard stories of catching fish by the cooler full, and I have also heard tales about "the one that got away." I recently heard a story from a friend who ended up with an angry manatee on his line. I have heard all kinds of fishing stories throughout my life, but I have never heard a fishing story about mending nets. It is not the glamorous part that anglers dreams about, but you cannot be consistently successful in catching fish without making time to mend the nets.

My father loves fishing, and some of my earliest memories as a young boy were going fishing with him. Whether it was fishing for Blue Gill on the quiet lakes of western Pennsylvania, or catching mullet and spot from the rickety pears of Topsail Beach, it was fun to be with dad doing something that he loved.

When I was really little, all I had to do to go fishing was wake up and go; but as I got older, I remember my dad bringing me into the workshop he set up in a storage room and explaining that part of being a fishermen was preparing your tackle and rods. We spent hours untangling line, refinishing old poles and making sure our reels were ready to go. My dad took time to show me which fishing lures worked in fresh water and which ones worked in the ocean.

My dad had all kinds of fishing poles. He had a stiff, twelve-foot surf rod that he said should be used only when we we're fishing from the beach. He had other rods that were good for fishing off of a pier, and some that were good for fishing out of boats. He even had one little "fly" rod that fit into a small canister. In addition to the rods, he had different tackle boxes that were full of bobbers, hooks and fancy lures. Each piece of tackle had a specific purpose, and he wanted me to know what they were for and how to use them. My dad taught me that there was a lot more to fishing than simply "casting nets." Good fishermen took time to be prepared.

I find it intriguing that Holy Spirit chose to let us know that James and John were mending nets on the day that Jesus called them. I believe it highlights two very important aspects of becoming fishers of men. The first is that it places an importance on the process of preparation.

The Greek word used for "mending" nets is *katartizō*. It is used thirteen times in the New Testament and means: "to render fit, sound or complete." In addition to mending, the word is translated as "perfect," "prepare," and "restore." It is also the root of the word "equip" found in the fourth chapter of Ephesians:

And He Himself gave some to be apostles, some prophets, some evangelists, and some pastors and teachers, for the equipping of the saints for the work of ministry, for the edifying of the body of Christ...

The process of preparing and equipping was and is a vital part of being a fisher of men. It was central to the life and ministry of Jesus, and is an essential part of practicing the culture of the few. For every great "sending story" recorded in the gospels, there were also "mending stories." Yes, it is more fun to think about being with the twelve as they returned rejoicing about seeing people healed and set free from the clutches of demons than to hear Jesus say, "How long do I have to be with you?"

The commitment of Jesus, the perfect Son of God, to walk and work with simple men who struggled to have faith is a beautiful demonstration of His perfect for love for us. In calling these fishermen from Galilee, Jesus chose men who would doubt Him, deny Him, and fall asleep in His greatest hour of need; yet He loved them until the end. Even as He was commissioning them before He ascended, Scripture tells us that some still doubted.

I have to admit; it is easier for me to think of the apostles as some kind of superheroes who really had it all together. The fact that they performed the same miracles that Jesus did has caused some theologians to set them aside as a different class of Christians. But then I read the stories of their weaknesses and fumbling and realize that they were a lot like me—imperfect men who had encountered the Perfect One. It was not their special abilities that allowed them to turn the world upside down; it was because they walked with and were loved by the One who entrusted them to carry the powerful message of the Kingdom of God.

He was the one with all of the power to change people's lives and restore all things to His Father.

the unexpected joys of mending nets

Over the past twenty years, I have had the privilege of being a part of several miraculous catches. There were times dozens or even hundreds of people came to Jesus within months or weeks. These were exciting indeed. But as we discussed earlier, when we bring people to Jesus without having a plan for discipling and equipping them, we leave them with an inferior encounter with the gospel. We say things like, "It is our job to catch them and God's job to clean them." The problem with this line of thinking is that if we leave our catch of fish lying unattended on the beach, the tide will come in and wash many back into the sea. While the process of sanctification is a work of the Holy Spirit, it is not disconnected from our call to make disciples.

The truth is, it is much easier to make converts than to make disciples. We must not stop at casting the nets. We need to make time for and place a value on the perfecting, restoring, and equipping process of discipleship. I finally came to this conclusion after being a part of four or five miraculous catches and realizing that there was little long-term change in many of the lives of people who had come to Jesus.

For me, I came to the proverbial tipping point the morning after witnessing one of the most amazing demonstrations of the power of the gospel I had ever seen. The story happened while we were living in Ellwood City, PA. Our primary focus during our time there was reaching out to addicts, some prostitutes, and many social orphans. We did this by engaging them where they lived, praying for people on street corners and in parks to experience the power and love of God—and it worked! Hearts were softened when people encountered God's undeniable power as they were healed and set free, and they were hungry to find out more.

One night, we had gathered twenty-five or thirty of these friends together to hear about Jesus. This was not a typical worship service. Most of these people were not only unchurched, they were anti-church. But they came that night to hear Sean's story.

Sean had been a practicing pagan who had been on his own since he was sixteen. I got to know Sean when he was nineteen. He was rough around the edges, but my wife saw something in him, something worth investing in. Sean was one of the more visible "social orphans" in our town. He was an easy target for all that was wrong and was frequently the target of accusations anytime an alley was vandalized or a store window was broken.

I remember being amazed as I looked around the room that night. Atheists, agnostics and anarchists had all come to hear what Sean would say. He was definitely not a polished speaker, but he was "one of them" and spoke their language. That night, Sean told them, in terms that they could relate to, how Jesus had changed his life. When he was done, another friend got up and briefly shared from Romans 1 about the power of the gospel.

I watched the reactions on people's faces as they heard the story of Jesus, some of them for the very first time. People who practiced looking hard and disconnected were crying and laughing listening to the story that night. Many of them responded to the invitation to accept Jesus, and God moved powerfully in our small gathering. Many were healed physically, experiencing the tangible sense of God's presence in ways they had never imagined possible.

Because these were not church people, they had no idea of proper protocol. I noticed that some of the ones who were accepting Jesus were leaving as soon as we finished praying with them. I didn't think much of it at the time. That all changed a few minutes later when they returned, bringing new people back with them. They were leaving to go find their friends. They went to parks and bars and to their neighbors' houses, telling whomever they could find that they needed to come meet this Jesus they had just encountered.

I was overwhelmed by how easily these brand new believers accepted the real, present reality of the gospel. Our little crowd had almost doubled as these new believers began doing the work of evangelists. I walked outside to get some fresh air, when I met one young woman who had literally run to the building. She was trying to catch her breath when she said to me, "My friend called and said Jesus was here, saving and healing people. Is He still here? Am I too late?"

I was wrecked by her question. I had been brought up with Jesus being the most important person in our household, but I was astonished and amazed by the childlike faith of this believing "unbeliever." I felt more aware of the reality of Jesus than I ever had in my life.

I woke up the next morning excited to call the pastors in our city. At that point in time, our ministry was functioning as an outreach, so I needed to find churches that would welcome these new believers in. At first, I was disappointed when I realized that my pastor friends were not quite as excited as I was by what had happened the night before. My disappointment grew to frustration and anger when I was told that their churches were not really set up to handle "those kind of people."

Borderline indignant, I began to pray. "God, what is wrong with these churches? Why don't they want these precious people?" I was just about ready to call fire down from heaven when I heard the Holy Spirit say, "Why are you angry at other people for not wanting to do what I called you to do?"

That question stopped me in my tracks. I remembered that for several years, we had been telling people that God had called us to Ellwood City to be and do church for people who would not come to church. I realized that I had become busy and was caught up casting nets, but had not prepared a place for the catch.

That was a turning point in my life. It was no longer enough to just have cool fishing stories; it was time to focus on preparing a net. I remember telling God that day, "Never again do I want to be a part of seeing people come to Jesus without knowing how we will love them and disciple them."

Since then, I have had the incredible privilege of discipling, equipping, and sending out some of the most stunning people on the planet. God has changed my heart, and now I know that there is incredible satisfaction in committing to walking with people through the hard things in life. As I have given myself to the "mending nets" part of the process, I have witnessed God restore dignity to women whose lives had been filled with shame. I have been able to help boys grow into men, and then watch them grow into godly husbands.

We have helped train people to follow Jesus, make disciples, and plant simple expressions of church on college campuses, in their neighborhoods, and in the nations. But more than training people to cast nets, we have been able to teach them how to value the process of loving people and committing to walk with them through the hard things of life.

I mentioned earlier that there were two important things we could take away from the fact that James and John were mending nets. The first was that it highlighted the importance of the preparation process. The second thing that I believe is relevant is that both the "casters" and the "menders" were recognized as fishermen, and they were all called to leave their nets to become fishers of men.

While it is true that God has gifted each of us in unique ways, we should never hide behind our gifting. Some of us thrive at the mending part of fishing but struggle to spend time with people who don't know Jesus. It is important that we do not stay in our comfort zone, but remember to make room to intentionally invest our lives with the lost. It is a part of following Jesus. And for those of us who find it easy to share our faith with people, but struggle to commit to the long, messy process of discipling someone, it is imperative that we follow the example that Jesus modeled in tenaciously loving His imperfect disciples to the very end.

I would like to challenge every would-be world-changer to examine the life of Jesus, and ask Him to help your heart grow to a place of dissatisfaction with any view of following Him that does not include both casting and mending nets. Both the catching and mending of men were a part of His life, and they are both an essential part of living out the culture of the few.

catching in community

Before we leave our fishermen friends, there is one last observation I would like to point out: In all of the fishing stories that we read in the Bible, we find no mention of a fishing pole. As far as I know, fishing poles didn't exist during the days of Jesus. All fishermen used nets.

Because things have changed in our culture today, I think it is easy for us to categorize the calling of Andrew, Peter, James and John as the calling of four individuals. But Jesus didn't approach them as individuals and say, "I will make you to become a fisher of men." He approached two sets of brothers and said, "I will make you *fishers* of men."

The fact that these men fished with nets meant that there are always at least two fishermen involved in every story. Having a fishing pole would have allowed Andrew to go solo, but that wasn't the case.

I think there is a high value in applying this principal to becoming fishers of men. In every story where we see Jesus sending out His disciples, He sends them out in pairs. Throughout the rest of the New Testament, we continue to see people being sent out to preach the gospel in pairs or in teams.

This is not accidental. While it does not take a village to disciple an individual, it is important that we learn to make disciples within the context of community. Regardless of our passion for reaching the lost, it can become extremely draining when we try making disciples on our own.

Remember, we want to develop a culture where people do more than say a quick prayer to receive Jesus. We want to see them discipled, equipped and sent out to then go make disciples themselves. The culture of the few calls for a commitment to building deep relationships with those we are discipling. One of the things that I have learned along the way is that it is easier to be excellent at disciple making when all of the pressure does not rest on me.

Every one of us will have days that we cannot be completely accessible to those we are discipling. We will avoid compassion fatigue and burnout if we have a "fishing buddy" that can help us when our plate gets full, or we simply need some time away.

Please do not underestimate the importance of building a culture of disciple-making around you. As you give yourself to inviting others to follow Jesus, it should become natural for those people to become disciple-makers themselves. This takes time, but it is worth waiting for.

If you don't know anyone that you can have as a fishing buddy, pray and ask God to send you someone. It might be someone who doesn't know Jesus yet or someone who has been a believer for a long time. Either way, take time to encourage each other and to regularly pray for people who don't know Jesus together. The old statement really is true: you can run faster alone, but you will run farther together.

Jesus started with his few. Most of them would have known each other well, had a lot in common, and would have already known how to work together. He chose men whose qualifications to lead the church did not come through their formal training, but from spending their lives together with Jesus.

Now when they saw the boldness of Peter and John, and perceived that they were uneducated and untrained men, they marveled. And they realized that they had been with Jesus. [10]

History tells us that this handful of brothers, neighbors and fishermen turned their world upside down with the message of Jesus, the cross, and the Kingdom of God. After 2000 years, Jesus is still calling men and women to follow Him and become fishers of men. It's our turn to walk with Him, give our lives to those who do not know Him, and turn our world upside down.

So far, we have looked at how Jesus knew His *identity* and lived with a spirit of invitation as He walked the earth. Next, we will look at the *intentionality* of Jesus to see exactly how He invested Himself in His disciples. This third key is an important part of cultivating a disciple-making culture, where others can join you in following Jesus and changing your world.

SECTION III
intentionality

9

redefining success

The third key to the *Culture of the Few* is *intentionality*, and I submit to you that Jesus modeled this more than any other person throughout history. The way He lived, investing into a handful of ordinary men, is the gold standard of how leaders can multiply themselves in the lives of others. If we want to know how cultural transformation really happens, then looking at the way Jesus intentionally interacted with people that He came in contact with is the perfect case study.

Over the last several chapters, we looked at the way Jesus related to those He called to follow Him. In this section, we will look at how He interacted with those He came in contact with on a daily basis. Whether He is teaching the multitudes or talking with Nicodemus alone on a rooftop, Jesus allows His life to be directed by looking at what the Father is doing and co-operating with Him to see that happen on the earth.

In this section we will also look at how living intentionally affects the way we look at success. One of the greatest challenges that world-changers face is that it is easy to have specific expectations of what success should look like that are not connected to seeing what the Father is doing. I was reminded of this several years ago when a friend of mine invited me to come to a conference that he was leading in a nearby city.

When I got to the venue, I got a close up view of the event from backstage. The blaring music was fresh, passionate, and performed with excellence. I had never seen the kind of white out effect that the light show was creating. I eventually moved to the back of the venue and saw that the show was as equally impressive as it had been from backstage. These people knew what they were doing.

They loved Jesus and were making a big impact on the church culture of America. I had been honored at the invitation to come spend the day with my friend and his team. Everything that I saw was completely legit. Everything I know about my friend and his ministry points to the fact that these people are authentically following Jesus and making a big impact for Him.

At the end of the night, after an amazing day of worship, teaching and equipping, my friend stood in front of several thousand people to wrap up the event. The crowd was excited, hoping somehow that the day could be extended just a little longer. Maybe the sun could stand still. This seemed so good.

My friend then told the crowd, "It's been great being here. Please stay connected through the website. Hope to see you next year. Good night." He then exited stage left.

In that moment, my heart was reminded of several things. First, my friend had brought his team to this city, thousands of miles from his home because they love Jesus and want to make Him famous. They were faithful in stewarding their opportunity to encourage several thousand youth and young adults in their walks with Jesus. Their worship and teaching were like fuel to hungry hearts—hearts that were ready to see the Kingdom of God come on earth as it is in heaven.

The other thought that ran through my mind was seeing how easy it would be for the crowd to look at this event and think, "This is what it looks like to change the world." Most in the crowd didn't know the years of faithful discipleship and prayer that my friend and his team had lived out away from the bright lights of the stage. What the crowd had witnessed over the past several days was the fruit of years of intentionally following Jesus together.

a different kind of excellence

I hope that the words that I have already written communicate that I see a definite Kingdom value in events like the one my friend invited me too. Conferences, camps, and all-day prayer gatherings can all be powerful. In general, though, I believe that lives are not most often changed in stadium crusades. Lives are changed in the midst of the ordinary things that happen in our lives every day.

To see cultural transformation take place in your neighborhood, campus or city there must be both fuel and function. The function is the way that we live out the fuel. It should be simple and reproducible, something that could be lived out in the biggest city or the smallest town. The *function* should not be a program or a club, it should be(come) a lifestyle that works as well with your next door neighbor as it does at a Sunday morning worship gathering. I believe that the function of learning how to follow Jesus in everyday ways is important because it represents how we will spend the majority of our lives.

If you are like most would be world-changers, embracing the values of *Culture of the Few* will most likely mean that your definition of success will need to be adjusted. It is not that having an arena packed with worshippers is *not successful*; it just does not define what success looks like. If we are going to follow Jesus, then we have to measure our lives as He measured His. His commitment to doing only what He saw the

Father do shaped how He spent every day of His life, and how He spent His every day should become the model for how we spend ours.

holding Jesus in the gutter

My wife, Adriane, is an amazing woman. I am so grateful to God for bringing us together. She has always had a heart for the hurting, and she loves giving to and serving the poor. While there are many different ways to engage the poor, for a season, we were regularly taking time to feed people that were hungry. Whether it was through a weekly soup kitchen in our town, or by going out looking for the hungry on the streets, there was something that came alive in my wife's heart when she engaged in serving others.

Adriane's passion to love others served as a way for Jesus to reveal Himself to me. As we looked for ways to remember Jesus in the everyday, I found myself finding Him in the eyes of those we were serving. Whether it was a homeless veteran living under a bridge, or a mentally challenged woman struggling through a harsh winter, I was regularly humbled as I remembered the Scripture: *Assuredly, I say to you, inasmuch as you did it to one of the least of these My brethren, you did it to Me.*[11]

I encountered this truth in a memorable way on one particular occasion. I was leading a team that was going out to feed the homeless on the streets in Pittsburgh. My sister Amy and I left our little town and made the 45-minute drive into the city, both of us ready for an adventure with Jesus. We daydreamed out loud about the possibilities of what God might do that night. Both of us sensed that we were on a special assignment from Jesus.

---

11   Matthew 25:40

In the midst of following Jesus in everyday ways within our sphere of relationships, we also recognized the need to follow Him into intentionally going out to seek those who needed to encounter Him. What would this look like? Would blind eyes open up on the street? Would missing limbs grow back? We could picture ourselves sharing the gospel right on the streets and dozens, even hundreds of people coming to Jesus.

With these expectations overflowing from our hearts, you can imagine our confusion when we got to Pittsburgh and had a hard time finding anyone to connect with. There were no takers for our free pizza and fried rice. We went to all of the normal spots and found no one. In fact, we ended up sending most of the team back home.

Amy and I decided to make one last run through Market Square, where many drifters usually hung out. We were excited to find about a dozen people there, all excited to eat some food. "Finally," I thought, "We can get on with our special assignment."

I began to talk with people, just to get a feel for the crowd and how the night was going. I didn't see any blind people, nor did I find anyone missing limbs. I did see one "little boy" sitting in the gutter. As I started to walk towards the gutter, I overheard the others talking about the police coming through and how it was time to leave.

I sat down next the "little boy" and discovered that it was really a woman in her forties. She was a user, and that night she was particularly wasted. All of her "friends" were leaving, and I was left trying to find out who this woman was and where she belonged. I learned that her name was Carol and that she was staying at a homeless shelter in town. I also found out that Carol couldn't go back to the shelter if she was intoxicated, which she definitely was.

So, with all of her "friends" scattering away from the coming police, I sat there in the gutter holding Carol. In that moment, I heard the Holy Spirit reminding me: *As often as you do it unto the least of these, you have done it to me.* I was undone, crying in the gutter thinking, "I am holding Jesus in the gutter..."

Now that I saw Carol as Jesus, the option of leaving her to fend for herself was completely gone. By this time, Amy and I were the only ones from our team left. We decided to load "Jesus" into Amy's car and set off to find some safe place for her to stay.

Carol was passed out from her drunkenness. She appeared to be folded over in the front seat of the car. As we drove around the streets of Pittsburgh, a city that I love, my eyes were opened to the brokenness that filled the streets in the night. Prostitutes walked the avenues and boulevards, addicts stood together shooting up in alleys, and the rest of the town slept, seemingly unaware.

Amy and I talked about how our "special assignment" hadn't worked out exactly as we had planned. But here we were, driving "Jesus" around in Amy's car, looking for a place for Carol to stay. We had gone through all of the known options and were completely out of ideas. It was just past one o'clock when we decided to make one last run through Market Square.

I am not entirely sure why I decided to drive back through the square, but when we got there I was relieved to see someone that I thought I recognized as a worker from a local men's shelter. "He might know of somewhere," I thought.

As I got out of the car to go talk to the man, Carol stirred. She was dazed, confused and suddenly aware of the fact that she needed to use the restroom.

As I approached the shelter worker I heard Amy frantically calling from the backseat. I turned around in time to see Carol pull down her pants and sit down on the edge of Amy's car. The thought that ran through my mind was, "Jesus is peeing in Amy's car!"

After we got Carol taken care of and back in the car, the man from the shelter told us that he did know of one place that might take Carol. He climbed into the car with us, and we headed for a boarding house on the North Side that he said would sometimes take in the homeless.

I can't explain what happened next, but it was real for both Amy and I. As soon as the man got out of the car to go check about the boarding house, both my sister and I knew that we would not see him again. We both looked up and saw that we were sitting right in front of the entrance to a hospital emergency room.

I looked at the clock. It was 1:42 AM. I told my sister, "If he is not back at 1:50, we are going to take her to the ER and see if there is anything they can do for her."

For the next eight minutes we sat in silence, both of us unaware that we were seeing the same thing. I am not sure if it was what people call an "open vision" or not, but we both began to see a replay of the day's events. Detail by detail, we retraced how the day had unfolded and how that unfolding had led us to this precise place at this precise time.

The clock hit 1:50, and the replay was over. I drove across the street and up to the entrance of the ER. I stopped and got Carol out of the car. As we put her into a wheel chair, a security guard pointed out where we could park the car while he wheeled her inside.

We prayed as we parked the car, both of us sensing that we had not missed our special assignment, but that it was just beginning. As we walked to the ER entrance, an ambulance was unloading a young man on a stretcher. We were not paying close attention to what was happening with him, but there was a sense that things were serious.

We walked into the Emergency Room and helped Carol get through triage. The nurse thanked us, and said that Carol probably had alcohol poisoning and that it was good that we had brought her in. As we turned to leave, a doctor came out of the ER and asked us if we were with the "Smith" family. We told him that we were not, and pointed him to a room where we had seen some family members gathering.

Before we could get out of the hospital, we heard screams come from the room. It was obvious that the doctor had delivered the ultimate bad news to a family in a waiting room at an ER. Their loved one had not made it. At the same time that we heard the screams, we looked up to see a young girl walking towards us from the opposite direction of the room.

She looked confused and disheveled. There was blood on her sweatshirt and her hair was a matted mess, but what really stood out was the loneliness in her eyes. She was right there, yet she seemed a million miles away. In that moment, the chaotic screams from the room behind us met up with the lost confused girl before us. We were caught right in the middle.

"It was you, you killed him. This is all your fault!" An angry voice sounded out from behind us. I turned and saw an obviously distraught mother coming towards the lonely girl in the hallway of the Emergency Room. A family member held her back and pulled her back in the room.

Without saying a word, the girl in front of us broke down crying and ran out the doors into the parking lot. Amy looked at me, knowing that although it was very different from what we had originally thought, that we had most definitely been given a special assignment from Jesus.

Amy followed the girl outside. I turned to try to find out more about what had happened so we could know how to help. The story was tragic. The girl had been at home with her boyfriend. He had been drinking when they got into an argument. There in his bed, he took out a gun and to spite her, he shot himself in the head.

The blood on her sweatshirt was his. The mess in her hair was the brains of her now dead boyfriend. No one could fault the anger that the boy's mother felt, but her angry outburst had sent this lonely girl out to edge of the parking deck. There, the same evil spirit that had convinced her boyfriend to take his life was now inviting this girl to do the same.

That is where I found Amy, at the edge of the parking deck. For the next hour, we held this girl, a perfect stranger. We cried with her, trying to speak life to her as the spirit of suicide told her that it would be better if she just ended it all.

At the end of the hour, a family member came and comforted her. With her parents only a few minutes from the hospital, we finally left at a little after 3 AM. The first part of our drive was quiet. Then we started crying, overwhelmed by the events of the last hour.

The daydreams of seeing a signs and wonders outbreak in the streets of Pittsburgh seemed so far away from what happened that night. There were no happy crowds, rejoicing with us in seeing our "special assignment" carried out. Yet our hearts were aware that we had been entrusted with caring for someone that was precious to Jesus in the darkest moments of her life.

I don't know if it is theologically correct to say this, but that night I felt gratitude from Jesus. It was like He was thanking us for loving Him and holding Him in the gutter and for being there for the lonely girl. I remember feeling so honored that Jesus entrusted these pearls of great price into our care for a short time.

I don't know what happened to Carol or to the lonely girl, but I do know that my life was changed forever that night. I began to have a deeper understanding that what looks like success in the eyes of man does not necessarily look the same in the eyes of heaven.

The Holy Spirit was messing with my image of success. It would have certainly been a great thing if the blind had received their sight back or the lame would have been restored that night. Had we had the chance of leading dozens of people to encounter Jesus on the streets, it would have been amazing. But what the Lord had for us that night was an invitation to be faithful in loving the ones that He brought across our path.

breaking the ruler

A lot of what I learned from Jesus, Carol, and the lonely girl that night was the value that God places on one life. That message was very clear to me yet, at the same time, hard for me to swallow. I was, after all, a history-maker and world-changer with big plans. Why wouldn't God want to release me to do "big things" for Him?

Again, let me be clear: I am not against those "big things." I feel so humbled by all the ways that I have been able to witness God revealing Himself. Sometimes it is in large crowds in spectacular fashion, but other times it has been completely different. The way that He shows up for the lonely single mother is just as "big" as when He multiplies food for the masses.

The truth is, He is always amazing. His love is always perfect. My view of what success looks like needs to be connected to recognizing what the Father is doing in a moment and then cooperating with Him in that moment. In recognizing my need to let Him set the priorities for what life should look like on a daily basis, I realize that my expectations of success are often based on an exceptional experience instead of on the glorious beauty of seeing Him work in normal, everyday ways.

In reflecting on what happened with Carol and the lonely girl that night, I discovered that in wanting to see the feeding of the five thousand type of moments become the norm in my life, I was overlooking what was really normal in the life of Jesus. Throughout the gospels we see over and over again stories of Jesus stopping for the one that was in front of Him. At times, he even seems to avoid the crowds in order to love and give Himself to the handful that He was talking to. What I began to notice is that it was not that Jesus didn't minister to the crowds, but that He did not allow the crowds to determine how He ministered to individuals.

As we move into the next chapter, we will look at the way that Jesus interacted with Zacchaeus and the woman at the well. In both of these stories, the way Jesus interacted with the individual had an impact on whole pockets of people.

10

everyday epic

One of the things that I most love about the life of Jesus is that we never see Him inviting anyone to anything other than Himself. I find this astounding. Even when we see Him ministering to the masses, it is His person that draws them close.

I believe that the way Jesus and His friends lived out their lives on a daily basis carried such a strong invitation with it that people found themselves longing to gather round this group of Galileans. It was the lifestyle of Jesus that attracted the crowds. Like I mentioned before, Jesus was always able to love and minister to an individual without allowing the presence of a crowd to distract Him.

I believe that Jesus did this because He knew that reaching an individual is key to reaching a whole pocket of people. This is an important part of the culture of the few. As the ultimate agent of change, Jesus recognized the influence individuals possess. As we look at the stories of Zacchaeus and the woman at the well, we will see that Jesus makes himself available to these individuals, who, in turn, would impact their own spheres of relationship.

the zacchaeus factor

Now behold, there was a man named Zacchaeus who was a chief tax collector, and he was rich. And he sought to see who Jesus was, but could not because of the crowd, for he was of short stature. So he ran ahead and climbed up into a sycamore tree to see Him, for He was going to pass that way. And when Jesus came to the place, He looked up and saw him, and said to him, "Zacchaeus, make haste and come down, for today I must stay at your house."[12]

I love the story of Zacchaeus because it is such a great example of how we see Jesus sharing the good news about the Kingdom. As Jesus was passing through Jericho, nothing seemed to be out of the ordinary. We have no record of gospel tracts or any type of an evangelistic outreach. He was simply walking through town. As He did, He became aware of the fact that someone was watching Him.

We do not know very much about Zacchaeus, but what we do know gives us insight into his life. He was a rich man, and those riches came at the expense of those he collected taxes from. He was probably not very popular among the people of Jericho.

Zacchaeus seems to have had a lot of reasons to have a chip on his shoulder. Here was a short, rich, probably unpopular tax collector, but somehow he had heard about Jesus and wanted to see him. What he does next is somewhat astounding to me because it certainly would have attracted attention from the people who most likely despised him.

As Zacchaeus climbed the sycamore tree that day, he had no idea that he was making himself a candidate for Jesus to single him out. But that is exactly what Jesus did. He looked for who was looking and invited Himself into their lives. This is a great example of how Jesus intentionally invested himself into the lives of people that He met in the midst of his everyday life.

---

12   Luke 19:2-5

It is easy to forget that Jesus did not have a script when he woke up that morning that told Him, "Today you are going to Zacchaeus' house." No, Jesus was simply walking through town, recognizing the spiritually hungry around him. I believe that one of the most important things we can do in sharing the good news about Jesus is to live our lives in a way that attracts the spiritually hungry and then learn to recognize that hunger.

Jesus did not invite Zacchaeus to come down from the tree and go to a church service. He invited himself into Zacchaeus' life. This caused a problem with the religious sector. They wondered how this great teacher could be the guest of such a sinner.

dinners with sinners

Several years ago, our simple church was reading through the Gospel of Luke and came across this story. I was impressed by the way that Jesus invited himself into the lives of people that He encountered. I also recognized that when I met people that needed Jesus, I rarely invited myself into their lives, but instead invited them to some Christian event. I became convicted by this and started encouraging my friends (and self) to look for who was looking at our lives and begin inviting ourselves into theirs lives. We came up with a fictitious program called "dinners with sinners" and began to pray for God to make these divine appointments happen.

While I grasped the concept of inviting myself into other people's lives, it made me extremely uncomfortable. All of my life I have been taught to protect my reputation. Now I was being confronted by the fact that if I was going to follow Jesus, I would have to lay down my own reputation in order to become friends with 'sinners.'

While I had taught about Jesus' interaction with Zacchaeus rather excitedly, I was somewhat hesitant to live it out. Thankfully, one of the young men that I was discipling was pretty insistent that we practice what we were learning. As we looked to see who was looking, there had been a family that had come to the soup kitchen we were operating that was obviously going hungry. Although the family was deeply broken, their hearts began to soften after the mother and one of the daughters received physical healing.

My young friend encouraged me to follow through and invite myself to dinner at their house. Their house was a scary place. In fact, it was known throughout our town as a place of spiritual darkness. I honestly did not want to go there, but knew that we needed to.

When we knocked on their door late one Thursday evening, I could feel butterflies in my stomach. I was quite content with the casual interactions that I had had with this family at the soup kitchen. Now, I was leaving an environment that I controlled to see if the gospel worked in the midst of their darkness. When Libby, the mom, opened the door, I could see that she was just as uncomfortable as I was.

This was the type of house that attracted the broken. In addition to the mom and her three daughters, there were always drifters and outcasts going in and out. My friend and I sat with this family for the next 45-minutes, watching people try not to swear while they figured out why we had come to their house. At the end of our time there, I asked if we could bring some pizza and come over for dinner the following week. They said yes, and I left having scheduled my first "dinner with sinners."

That dinner never happened, however, because just a few days later one of Libby's daughters had a seizure. The paramedics were called, and when they came to the house they found deplorable living conditions. I received a frantic phone call from one of the daughters informing me that Child Protective Services told her mother that unless their house was in good order by the end of the week, the state would take the children.

All of a sudden, I became very thankful for the persistence of my young friend. The timing of our visit to their home made them feel safe enough to reach out to us and ask for help in this hour of need. Within 24 hours, we mobilized our small simple church to help this precious family clean out their house. Three days and two dump trucks later, it was back in working order.

As we we finished cleaning on the last day, I remember standing out in front of the garage when Libby came up and gave me a hug. With tears running down her cheeks, she looked up at me and asked if we could start one of our "little churches" at her house. Over the next three months, over 50 people gave their lives to Jesus at a church plant in Libby's garage.

Just like in the story of Zacchaeus, salvation came to Libby's house. I was humbled by the way that Jesus showed up to pour out healing and deliverance at that little simple church. Good things happen when we follow Jesus in engaging people with the good news where they live.

touching the untouchables

While my heart was excited to see the message of Jesus impact the lives of Libby's family and friends, there was still something that felt uncomfortable to me. I was being confronted by the reality of seeing the gospel work really well with people that I had spent a lifetime trying to avoid. The more I thought about it, the more I realized how easy it had been for me to discriminate in whom I shared Jesus with.

The little simple church that met Libby's house was filled with the broken, lonely and tired. As I saw the power of God impacting these precious people, I was reminded of the fact that while their needs were more visible and obvious to the onlooker, that I was just as much in need of the active, powerful message of the good news to transform my life. I am so thankful that my friend forced me to go to Libby's house that night. It was more than me following through on a teaching, it was an important part of me learning to follow Jesus.

Not only did Jesus identify with sinners when He stepped into line to be baptized, but He spent much of His life knowing and becoming known by those that were culturally undesirable. Time after time, Jesus eats with the wrong people, intervenes on behalf of the guilty and allows sinners to touch Him in ways that made the religious whisper. He never allowed His righteousness to become a barrier from interacting with the untouchables of His day. Jesus engaged people where they lived with a radical love that reached out to them, while never compromising.

Learning to follow Jesus in this area was difficult for me. It went against my desire to be respectable. Over the last few years I have learned that as long as we feel a need to be respected by others, it will be very difficult for us to follow the One who made Himself of no reputation.

Reading the gospels will show us that Jesus consistently gave Himself to those that society had very little value for. He became friends with harlots, dined with tax collectors, and touched lepers. He intentionally made himself available to the lost parts of the society of His day. In fact, He said it was for these people that He had come.

I have so much respect for the way that Jesus never allowed His reputation to get in the way of love. Though it drew the ire of the religious rulers, Jesus was consistent in stopping for the least of these wherever

He went. Day by day, He extended Himself to the broken in the midst of everyday life.

A woman of Samaria came to draw water. Jesus said to her, "Give Me a drink." For His disciples had gone away into the city to buy food. [13]

On the surface, this conversation doesn't seem very significant; but the fact that Jesus was interacting with a woman from Samaria was enough to surprise her. Jews did not like Samaritans. In fact, they looked down on them as half-breeds. To go beyond this cultural barrier, it was even less common for a Jewish man to interact with a Samaritan woman.

As you read John 4, there is no mistaking the fact that this woman, who was in the midst of an everyday task, was stunned to be having a conversation with Jesus. It is also worth noting that Jesus started the conversation by simply asking for a drink of water. He did not do this as a clever evangelism technique; Scripture says that He was tired and thirsty.

Once again, Jesus is making the most of everyday opportunities. When the woman at the well began to interact with Him, He immediately began speaking about the living water that He had to offer. What started as a simple request for water was quickly turning into a life-changing experience.

As Jesus talks about a water that would satisfy a person forever, the woman says, "Sir, give me this water." Jesus looks deep into her life and tells her to go call her husband. When the woman exclaims that she has no husband, Jesus goes deeper yet again.

You have well said, 'I have no husband,' for you have had five husbands, and the one whom you now have is not your husband; in that you spoke truly.[14]

Shocked by how Jesus could know such a thing about her, the Samaritan woman dove into a discussion about spirituality. The prophetic nature of what Jesus had spoken to this woman had accessed her heart. It was in the midst of this conversation that Jesus reveals Himself to her as Messiah.

Later in the chapter, we find that this untouchable woman had been touched by Jesus. She returns to her town and begins to tell them all about the man who "told me everything I ever did." The Bible says that many believed because of her testimony.

The whole town was impacted because of the way that Jesus interacted with one woman who was in the midst of an everyday task. This is the very essence of culture of the few: that many were able to drink of the Living Water because of the way Jesus loved the one. It almost seems too good to be true.

don't lose the everyday in the epic

It is my hope that as we have looked at these amazing stories of Jesus showing up in the midst of everyday life, your hearts are stirred more to change the world. His life show us that we don't have to choose between the ordinary moments and the extraordinary ones, but that the extraordinary moments are often found in the midst of the ordinary ones. Don't lose the epic in the everyday, or the everyday in the epic.

I believe that as we are faithful to intentionally follow Jesus into everyday encounters, we will find ourselves in the midst of our own

14   John 4:17-18

epic stories of how Jesus is making Himself known. And making Him known is what really matters.

I remember a conversation that I had with some friends who were getting ready to go to a restricted access nation. They were young college students who had been praying and reaching out to some refugees in their city. As they had been praying and following Jesus in everyday life, the doors began to open up to build relationships with people from this country that had been closed to the gospel for years.

I was talking to them as they were on their way to the airport. We were praying together, asking God to bless their time in the country. The conversation shifted when we realized that this was a very special opportunity to take the gospel to a place where most people had never even heard the Name of Jesus.

My heart became aware of a spiritual tension that I don't think I had ever seen before. This was truly an epic opportunity, but it came about because a small group of people had been following Jesus in their everyday lives. It is important to recognize that Jesus has a way of displaying His glory in the most ordinary things.

Recognizing that the most epic stories in the gospel usually start with ordinary things like a few loaves and fishes will help us learn how to maximize the everyday moments where Jesus is waiting to show up. We will continue to build upon this idea as we complete this section on intentionality by talking about the importance of learning to be present in the places where we do life.

11

dwelling in the land

"By faith he dwelt in the land of promise..." —Hebrews 11:9

When we walk with Jesus and live our lives in a way that we see the gospel work in the midst of the "everyday," we become dangerous to darkness. Because we carry the seed of Christ with us wherever we go, a trip to the grocery store can have just as much impact as a mission trip to a third world country. When we recognize this, our perspective will change as our lives becomes a ministry from Jesus to the world around us.

This kind of living requires an ongoing, growing belief that God is passionate about reaching every tribe, nation and tongue. It doesn't stop me from becoming a missionary to a restricted access nation, but it does empower me to live out the mission of the gospel wherever I am.

I remember seeing this truth demonstrated powerfully in the summer of 2010 on the Southside slopes of Pittsburgh, PA. We were hosting a two-week missions training school (Student CPx) where college students would be trained to make disciples and live like missionaries on their campuses. Our original plan was to hold the school on one of the area college campuses, but some last minute logistical changes "forced us" to relocate to the Burning Bush—an old Catholic monastery in the city.

A monastery with ornate statues and a chapel with thirty-foot ceilings was the last place I would have chosen to host a training school that was equipping people to plant "simple churches," but as we were limited in our options, I was willing to consider. So Adriane, my friend Jessie and I drove down to check it out, and as we did, we recognized that relocating our school from the campus into the city was not an accident. We were all aware that God was leading us to this place, this exact neighborhood, for our time of training.

As the start of the school approached, the confirmation continued. One of our team members, a stellar young woman named Lindsay, shared with us that God had been speaking to her from Psalm 37. Verse three had been having a particular impact on her. "Trust in the Lord, and do good; dwell in the land, and feed on His faithfulness."

Lindsay shared what she was learning with us during the first several days of our missions school. She told us about how God had been helping her grow to love the neighborhood and neighbors around where she was living. This was saying something for Lindsay, who had spent the previous two years traveling, ministering in powerful ways from campus to campus here in the United States, as well as internationally.

Lindsay's message had a real impact on our students. The simple commission to "dwell in the land" became an oftheard motto as students talked about how they planned to spend their time in the city. Students who came to SCPx with ideas of "taking the nations for Jesus" were now learning to see the real Kingdom value in being present where they were at the moment. God provided us with some real-life learning lab experiences during our time together in Pittsburgh.

One afternoon, a few of our students decided to practice "dwelling in the land" by playing basketball at a nearby park. After playing for a while they got thirsty, so they went to a local convenience store to get some juice. While they were there, they ended up in a conversation with a few other customers. They invited their "new friends" outside to continue the chat, and before it was over the new friends became new believers and were baptized in the park where our students had been playing basketball.

Jasmine, one of the "dwellers," called me that afternoon. She was so excited about what God had done in the midst of them taking the time to "just be" in the neighborhood. "I was just trying to buy juice," she had stated.

As followers of Jesus, we live with a mandate to disciple nations. One of the greatest purposes of my life is to live out that mandate and to equip others to live it out as well. That said, a part of the culture of the few is understanding that we need to be faithful in discipling our neighborhoods and cities before we try to take the nations. Jesus told His few to preach the gospel in Jerusalem and the uttermost parts of the earth.

My heart is genuinely saddened when I meet people who are ready to relocate to Africa or South East Asia to become missionaries, but they have never practiced making disciples and living out the gospel where they live. Some of them have explained to me that they are not called to make disciples here. Others have said that their hearts will be more alive in their dream destinations, so there will be more of a grace for them to live out the message there.

I want to encourage people to have a heart for the nations. But I believe that the greatest way to learn how to disciple the nations is to live out the gospel locally. We must never try to export missions someplace else if we have not integrated the mission of Jesus into where we do life now. I have seen so many young leaders unnecessarily suffer burnout and fatigue by rushing to get where they are going instead of learning how to dwell in the land.

an unthinkable strategy

"But Brad," you say, "You don't understand the urgency of the situation. The people in Zambia are dying without Jesus. We need to reach them now!" Please don't mistake what I am saying for passivity about seeing the gospel spread. The nations do need to hear the life-changing message of the gospel of the Kingdom of God, and we do need to acknowledge that there is a sense of urgency in meeting that need. But remember, God sees our present in the context of history and eternity.

I learned this by reading Jeremiah 29. As soon as some of you read the words 'Jeremiah 29,' verse 11 immediately popped into your heads.

For I know the thoughts that I think toward you, says the Lord, thoughts of peace and not of evil, to give you a future and a hope.

This is a great verse with a message of hope and encouragement for God's people. You can find it on posters, plaques and bumper stickers. It's so good to know that God is thinking nice thoughts about us. But have you ever noticed that there are no bumper stickers with Jeremiah 29:10 on them?

For thus says the Lord: After seventy years are completed at Babylon, I will visit you and perform My good word toward you, and cause you to return to this place.

Seventy years? Really?

Once I had read verse 10, I decided to go back and study the story around these verses. What I discovered was a God-given plan that seemed like a highly unlikely, unlikable solution for the problem that the children of Israel were facing. Please allow me to set the scene for you.

Jeremiah, the weeping prophet, had written a letter to the exiles who had been carried away from Jerusalem. They were being held hostage in Babylon. I can just imagine the excitement among the community of exiles when they heard that they had received a letter from the prophet. Would this letter bring a word from the Lord about how God would deliver His people?

I can almost see a Jewish woman wringing her hands trying to figure out what to do first. Should she begin packing her few belongings? Maybe she should get an early start on baking some bread for the coming journey.

The Bible does not tell us where the people assembled to hear the reading of the letter, but try to place yourself among the captives. I am sure there was a mixture of nervousness and excitement as one of the elders asked for everyone to settle down before the letter from the prophet of God was read. Quickly, the crowd was quieted. Ready. Waiting. Listening to hear God's plan to deliver His people from a wicked king in a pagan land.

"Thus says the Lord of hosts, the God of Israel," the elder began to read. "To all who were carried away captive, whom I have caused to be carried away from Jerusalem to Babylon..." Can you feel the uneasiness in the room as the exiles reflect on the words that explain God has a cause in their captivity?

Build houses and dwell in them; plant gardens and eat their fruit. Take wives and beget sons and daughters; and take wives for your sons and give your daughters to husbands, so that they may bear sons and daughters—that

you may be increased there, and not diminished. And seek the peace of the
city where I have caused you to be carried away captive, and pray to the Lord
for it; for in its peace you will have peace. [15]

I believe that the sounds of weeping and lamentations filled the
room as Jeremiah's letter was read, for in the letter, they discovered that
God's plan did not call for an immediate deliverance from Babylon. To
be clear, they were living in a nation and under the control of a king that
despised and mocked the Holy One of Israel. How could it be God's
plan to subject them to this culture?

Jeremiah's letter indicated that the deliverance of the people would
not soon come. In fact, there were instructions in the letter that spoke
of future generations. Instead of raising up another Moses who would
move in signs and wonders and deliver His people out of a bad situation,
God introduces a plan for the long haul. Let's take a look at the basic
instruction from the letter to see what we can learn for our day.

build a house | move in

Deliverance is the dream for hostages, so it is almost unthinkable
for an exile to spend much time in the real estate office. When you are
a slave, your dream house has little to do with the latest appliances or
the customization options of the floor plan. It has everything to do with
your homeland.

This first instruction would have been hard to swallow for the
Israelites who had been carried away to Babylon. In just a few words,
their understanding of their situation would have changed completely.
Instead of making escape plans, now they will need to pull building
permits. God was telling His people to construct houses, or dwelling
places, so to speak.

---

15   Jeremiah 29:5-7

The first part of God's instruction to these prisoners of war was to "dwell in the land." What a defeat this must of been to the hopes of the Jewish families. But what a revelation of God's heart for His people who find themselves forced to live as strangers in a foreign country.

Have you ever felt that the culture that you live in denies God? That it is built upon principles that contradict His Kingdom? Have you noticed how easy it is for us to pray for God to raise up a new leader to spare our nation, or that He would send "revival" to heal our land?

I am not against God raising up a deliverer, nor am I opposed to revival, but the Jeremiah story reminds us that sometimes God has a purpose in planting His people in the midst of broken culture as a way of establishing His presence there. Instead of looking for a deliverer to make things better, what would it look like for Jesus to be represented in our lives in the midst of the mess? It's easy to be so caught up looking for an escape hatch that we miss the cause of God in the midst of our situation.

When the people heard Jeremiah's letter, they were forced to come to terms with the fact that they were being called to dwell in the midst of a land that railed against their God. Likewise, Daniel and his friends were stripped of their identities and even their manhood in an attempt to indoctrinate them into the ways of Babylon. Yet in the midst of Godlessness, Daniel purposed in his heart to follow The Lord.

Daniel, Shadrach, Meshach and Abednego became powerful rulers, even though they were hostages. Through their authority, God displayed His majesty and glory to some of the wickedest rulers in the history of civilization. With their hearts still set on God and their homeland, these captives learned how to dwell in the land and make a difference there.

plant a garden | eat the fruit

If "building a house" speaks to dwelling in the land, then what can we learn from the instruction to plant gardens and eat of the fruit? I believe the process of breaking up the ground in a foreign land must have been equally as difficult and unnatural for the Jewish exiles as constructing houses. Gardening is not something that we begin today and benefit from tomorrow. It takes commitment and time to produce fruit that we can be nourished by. And that seems to be what God was asking of these exiles—commitment over time.

One year, when my daughter was in kindergarten, my wife decided that it would be a good learning experience for us to have a family garden. While I was quite sure that having a little garden in our tiny backyard was going to be a lot of work, I also agreed that it would be a good way for Abigail to learn, and it would be good for us to do it together.

We looked at the small space that we had available, and tried to figure out what should go into our garden. I remember going to the local hardware store and buying a few landscaping timbers to set the borders for our garden. I got home and began to mark out the space, which was only about one hundred square feet.

A friend had offered to bring over a rototiller to make things easier, but after three or four days of not hearing back from him, we realized that we were going to have to turn the soil the hard way. It didn't take long for the blisters to form on my hands from our little 24' by 4' garden. After just a few hours, my hands were bleeding and my back hurt. And, I was not even halfway done hoeing the garden.

I was digging up soil that had been nothing more than a backyard for decades. With every strike of the hoe, I was turning beautiful, established sod into broken ground. I distinctly remember thinking about how much Jesus talked about farming in His parables and gaining a new understanding of the process of the Kingdom of God.

I was ripping my backyard apart. Without the breaking up of the ground and the turning of the soil, the seed would have no place to go. It took me most of three afternoons and the help of a few friends to get the soil turned, but by Friday evening the ground was ready for planting.

Abigail was excited when we took her to the local gardening store on Saturday morning to get what we needed. We had decided to try to grow tomatoes, peppers, carrots, cucumbers, squash and watermelon. While we started this garden to give Abi a chance to learn, I am pretty sure that I was the one receiving the real education.

As I sat on the swing on our back porch reading the instructions that had come along with the seeds and plants, I was struck by how much I was learning about the need for order in our little garden. There were some plants that needed to be planted close to each other so they could cross pollinate and share nutrients. There were other plants that needed eighteen inches of distance from any other plant so they would have room to fully grow.

The tomatoes would eventually need staked. The cucumbers grew best if they could grow down a mound. I was astonished by all of the details I was learning about my future food, but what really got me was how much work it took to grow it. I had already invested a lot of time into our little learning project, yet gardening required a commitment that came without the guarantee of a good harvest.

Over the summer, I had the luxury of watching my garden from the swing on my back patio. While nothing seemed to happen quickly at first, soon we saw sprouts begin to grow. I remember how excited we all were to go back and water our garden in the early evening time. We would take time to watch the progress of every plant. We would count the grape tomatoes on each plant, patiently waiting for them to reach full maturity so we could pick them and enjoy them for dinner. Our homemade marinara sauce had never tasted so good as it did that summer, when we were enjoying the fruit from our own garden.

Can you imagine how difficult it would have been for the exiles to think about the amount of time and hard work that would have been required of them before they could enjoy any harvest? And as exiles, there wasn't even the guarantee that they would be able to keep their harvest if it was good. After all, they were slaves in a foreign land.

Planting a garden meant that they were committing time and hard work from the beginning of a growing season, that they would only enjoy if they endured until the harvest. Through every part of the process, they would have had to practice patience, with the hope that the fruit at the end would make it worthwhile. A successful harvest wouldn't change the fact that they were still in exile, but it would sustain them in the midst of it.

In spite of their circumstances and surroundings, there was something healthy about the children of God demonstrating fruitfulness. It can be easy to be overwhelmed by our surroundings and use our situation as an excuse not to bear fruit, but we were made to bear fruit. Jesus told us that fruit happens as we abide in the vine, regardless of the friendliness of our situation. As we learn to dwell in the land, I believe it is imperative for us to invest time and hard work into cultivating fruitfulness in our lives.

get married | make babies

While I think that the instruction to build houses and plant gardens were difficult for the exiles to hear, they spoke to the tangible needs that the people of Israel had. They needed places to live and they needed food to eat—even if their stay was only going to be temporary.

"Okay, so we will make a lean-to and plant a garden that will get us by until the end of the harvest. It's not what we were hoping for, but we can make it work for a few more months…" But then the prophet's letter moves on to the third part of the instruction.

Take wives and beget sons and daughters.

I believe that each part of Jeremiah's instructions revealed more about the long-term process that God was leading His people through, but none revealed more than this one. At this point, we are moving beyond providing for the immediate needs of food and shelter and into the process of starting families.

Remember, we are not talking about modern dating in Western culture; marriages in this culture were typically arranged, and with a great deal of preparation. The reading of the Old Testament stories about marriage sometimes sounds more like business transactions than love stories. From Jacob's plight of working for fourteen years for the right to marry Rebekah, to Boaz swapping shoes with the rightful kinsman redeemer to win Ruth, we know that there was a lot for a bride and groom to work through.

Typically, a Jewish groom would have 'prepared a place' in his father's house before going to get his bride. How could this happen while living in a foreign land as an exile? I believe that the instruction to get married and have children spoke volumes to those who were hearing Jeremiah's letter read. It said, "You're not going anywhere for a while…"

Starting a family would have required the Jewish people to start thinking of living out their future under their current circumstances. Again, this has much importance for us today. It can be so easy for us to want to wait until we have everything figured out before we truly begin to live. The words of the prophet to the people of God charged them to live out who they were in the midst of their hardship.

Perhaps nothing speaks more of the future than seeing young couples married and starting their families. It is in the process of consummation that the possibility of conception occurs. And what is conception other than the seed of the future being released into the present.

While the words of the prophet must have sounded strange at the time, in Jeremiah's commission to start families, he was really giving permission for the exiles to begin the process of their futures while they were being held captive. We must learn how to practice conceiving our future before we get there.

raise your kids | have grand kids

The final instruction of raising their families and marrying their children off "so that they may bear sons and daughters" added a sense of dimension to the longterm outlook that the prophet was speaking about. It spoke of future generations being born into captivity. Building off of the thought that we must learn how to begin engaging with our future before we get there, this instruction also came with the hope that the exiles would indeed have a future.

When we are surrounded by intimidating circumstances, it is easy to drift into a place of hopelessness. In fact, sometimes it is easier to assume that we will have no future at all than to contend and stand in the midst of adversity. Rarely are these intimidating circumstances as big as they appear, but when you are living in the midst of these moments, that can be hard to remember.

When I think back to that little Jewish woman who had entered into the room excited to hear the prophet's letter, it is easy for me to think that she would have been on the edge of hopelessness at the thought of raising her family in Babylon. Just a few minutes earlier she was trying to decide how to prepare for her journey home, and now she is faced with the reality that if she is to prepare to raise her grandchildren here in this place, then maybe she would never make it home at all.

It is in moments like these that we must hold on to the promises of God and pattern our lives to stand for those promises. That is what it means to live intentionally in the midst of chaos. Jesus promised us that we would encounter trials in this world, but that we could be of good cheer because He had overcome those trials. It is important for us to stay focused on His promise of a future, especially when it looks like we have none.

the promise of increase

The thought of seeing grandchildren born into exile must have been difficult, but with this fourth instruction, a clear sense of purpose was also given.

...and take wives for your sons and give your daughters to husbands, so that they may bear sons and daughters—that you may be increased there, and not diminished.[16]

God had a clear purpose and plan after all. He had not forgotten or turned His back on His people. Throughout the instructions of building houses, planting gardens and raising families, God had a good intention in His heart all along. Increase.

In the last instruction to raise families and have grandchildren, God was actually speaking to the exiles about His plan for raising up a deliverer. Generationally speaking, it is very possible that that grandfather of Mordecai and Esther would have been in the room when that letter was read.

This is incredible. Yes, Esther shows up "at such a time as this," but her grandparents were given instructions to simply dwell in the land and bring His presence there. God gave specific instructions to His people that required them to live intentionally for seventy years. But all along He was preparing the times and seasons to show His good plans to His people.

As we we conclude this section on intentionality, let's look at one more verse from Jeremiah 29.

And seek the peace of the city where I have caused you to be carried away captive, and pray to the Lord for it; for in its peace you will have peace. [17]

God has a plan to bless His people with peace. In fact, He already has. We have peace because we have been reconciled to God, and He has sent His Spirit to come dwell within us.

As we have received peace, I believe that we have both an invitation and a responsibility to release the peace of God into the culture around us. God spoke to the exiles to pray for and bless the city of their captivity. This is the heart of intentionality in the Culture of the Few, moving into a place of purposefully praying for and releasing the culture of heaven into people and places here on earth.

Like that little Jewish woman, Jesus was also born into a time when God's people where in captivity. The Jews of His day were under the rule of the Roman Empire. They were mistreated, oppressed, and in hope of a new deliverer. Only God did not send the warrior king that they were expecting, but introduced Messiah as a humble carpenter from Nazareth. It's worth repeating that out of the thirty-three years Jesus spent on the earth, He spent the first thirty away from the public eye, simply dwelling in the land.

As we look to Jesus as the ultimate agent of change, it is important for us to remember that the brokenness of the culture He was born into did not stop the goodness of the gospel of His life from spreading. In fact, His handful of ordinary friends would "turn the world upside down" within just a few years of His resurrection.

Following Jesus.
Transforming Culture.

Investing our lives into those around us to impact them in the midst of the everyday, despite the circumstances of our surroundings, is the essence of *Intentionality* within the *Culture of the Few*. As we move into the last two sections of the book, we will examine the topics of *Intercession* and *Intimacy* to see how Jesus lived His hidden life with the Father.

SECTION IV
intercession

12

invisible lifestyle

As we transition from looking at the way Jesus lived and invested His life intentionally into the lives of His few, it could seem like we have hit the climax of this book. That would be accurate if we only looked at the external ministry of Jesus, but as we journey on in *Culture of the Few* we will find that there was something happening behind the scenes of Jesus' life that is actually quite integral to our story.

Now in the morning, having risen a long while before daylight, He went out and departed to a solitary place; and there He prayed. [18]

Behind the scenes, under the surface, we see the forth and fifth keys to the *Culture of the Few* at work. *Intercession* and *Intimacy* were both key components of the lifestyle that Jesus lived out in the stories told to us in the gospels. These were the invisible, or hidden, parts of His life that allowed His public ministry to take place.

In some ways these two aspects of the life of Jesus go hand-in-hand. Like two strands of DNA that spiral together, they are structurally bound, yet run in opposite or "anti-parallel" directions. Intimacy is all about closeness with God. Intercession is focusing our prayers on others. Intimacy leads us into God's presence for seeking His Face, while Intercession leads us to pray prayers that are an outflow from His

Heart. In the same way that DNA forms the structure of our physical life, Intimacy and Intercession intertwine to form the structure of our spiritual life. The invisible lifestyle that we cultivate through seeking the face of God and praying the prayers of His heart reveal our spiritual code far more than our messages or miracles ever will.

For the purpose of this book, we will look at them each separately, but with an understanding that they flow together. First, we will take a look at *Intercession* as the fourth key to the *Culture of the Few*, understanding that the best intercession flows out of intimacy.

prayer: the most effective habit

In 1989, author Steven R. Covey released *The Seven Habits of Highly Effective People*. The book became wildly popular with business leaders and educators alike, making an impact in the way that thought-leaders approached the subjects of management and paradigm change. President Bill Clinton even invited Covey to Camp David to discuss how the content of the book could be applied to his presidency.[19]

The concept of Covey's work is not hard to understand. As revealed in the title, he simply looked for the habits or character traits that were common to successful people. When searching the life of Jesus we find many things to emulate, but perhaps one of the most practical is a regular rhythm of prayer and being with the Father. He was constantly making time to separate Himself from others and be alone with the God.

This "habit" of prayer is noteworthy, because Jesus didn't usually do the same thing twice. Reading the gospels, we notice that sometimes He healed a blind eye by making mud, while other times He spit into the eye itself—which makes sense if Jesus did not live according to a

---

19   Harper, Lena M. (Summer 2012). "**The Highly Effective Person**". *Marriott Alumni Magazine*. Retrieved March 21st 2016.

script, but only did what He saw the Father do. Yet we do see Him consistently slipping away to spend time with the Father to pray. Herein lies the perfect intersection between intimacy and intercession.

A standard definition of the word intercession is "acting on behalf of another." It is interesting to note that Jesus acted on the behalf of others in prayer as He communed with the Father. If we remember that Jesus is the exact representation of the Father on earth, then we will understand that Jesus was able to move into intercession for others because He was expressing agreement with what was on the Father's heart for people.

The word intimacy speaks to the "closeness" or familiarity that one has with another. I believe the primary reason that Jesus went away to spend time with the Father was because of the closeness that existed between them. We will expand upon this more in the section on Intimacy, but it is important that we touch on it now to understand the way that Jesus engaged in prayer and intercession. Jesus lived with a high level of commitment to an ongoing lifestyle of prayer, but it was as He pursued closeness with the Father that His intercession began.

the answer to prayer

I remember reading many years ago that "the answer to prayer is more prayer."[20] I really believe that. In my own life, I find that the more time I spend with God in prayer, the more my hunger for prayer grows. Because of this hunger that is produced in us as we spend time with the Father and learn to pray the prayers that are on His heart, the answer to prayer is fulfilled by being with Him.

This intermingling of intimacy and intercession is important for us to see. Many times we can associate the word *intercession* with intense warfare or the need to plead our case to God, trying to convince Him

20   Cymbala J. (2003). *Fresh Wind, Fresh Fire*. Grand Rapids, Michigan: Zondervan.

do what we are asking Him to do. While there is definitely a place for fervent, passionate prayer, we need to let that fervent passion arise from a heart that has been made aware of the throne room desires of the Father.

The prophet Isaiah pleaded with God to "rend the heavens" and come down.[21] There was a passionate desire in His heart for God to hear his prayer and reveal Himself. Later in his prayer, Isaiah says *"There is no one who calls on Your name, who stirs himself up to take hold of You."*[22]

Having a good perspective about prayer can actually propel us into God's presence with a holy fire to pursue and "take hold" of God. But if we miss the intermingling of intercession and intimacy, we can find ourselves praying passionate prayers to God without a clear understanding of His heart.

I learned this when I had traveled with some friends of mine to a "prophetic worship" gathering where one of my favorite worship leaders was ministering. I was so excited to road trip to our state capital and encounter God for the weekend. We arrived at the church where the conference was being held just in time to get "good seats." As things got underway, my heart was full of anticipation. There were hundreds of us ready to "press in" and "contend" in prayer. We were ready to bombard heaven for the release of God's power.

"God, rend the heavens and come down! Come do what You want to do! Oh, how we want You to come…"

As I prayed for God's glory to be released over the state capital, I remember praying for one of our friends who had not yet come to Jesus.

---

21   Isaiah 64:1
22   Isaiah 64:7

"God, save Sean. I cry out to you! Please come and do whatever you have to do to save Sean. We want Sean to be saved…"

I had been worshipping up front near the stage for 15-minutes or so when I sensed the Holy Spirit inviting me to abandon my "good seats" and move all the way to the back of the room. Begrudgingly, I grabbed my Bible and journal and walked to the very back of the large sanctuary and sat down against the wall.

"Okay, God, I am here. What do you want to say to me?"

I am very aware that I don't always hear God with 100% accuracy. After all, we know in part and prophesy in part. On this night, however, the Spirit of God made Himself very clear.

"Why are you praying the way you are praying?" He asked.

A simple question. I began to think back to my passionate prayers at the front of the room.

"Did you know that you will *never* want Me to come into a situation more than I already want to come? You will never want Me to save Sean, or anyone else, more than I want them to be saved. I already gave my Son for Sean. I love him so much…"

Tears began to roll down my cheeks as I sat against the back wall of that big sanctuary. The Spirit of God was taking me through an introductory class at the School of Prayer.

"I am glad that you are stirred up to pray, just don't overlook the desires of My heart as you do..."

What a life changing experience for me. I am not sure if I had ever really thought about the heart of God towards the things I was praying for. Maybe this was because intercession seemed more like a responsibility to me than an invitation into intimacy.

I had watched God answer prayers throughout my entire life. My mom and dad had done an excellent job of drawing my sisters and I into family prayer when we were younger. They let us know that God was our provider, and my dad kept a stack of index cards with Scripture promises of God's faithfulness in his desk drawer that he often pulled out and prayed from during our family prayer times.

"Ah, Lord God! Behold," my dad would read, a quiver in his voice and a tear in his eye. "Thou hast made the heaven and the earth by Thy great power and stretched out arm, and there is nothing too hard for thee."[23] My parents were courageous and vulnerable in allowing us to know the needs of our family. They were committed to showing off the power of God to do the impossible.

Many times, I had seen God fulfill the promise to do exceedingly and abundantly beyond what we could ask or think, but I am still not sure if I had ever really considered what His heart's desires were about the things that I was praying for. It is almost as if I thought that His heart's desire was just for someone to pray, so that He would have someone to answer.

---

23   Jeremiah 32:17 KJV

God is so gracious. He lovingly answered so many prayers that I had prayed to Him, but that night, He showed me that He also wanted to answer prayers that I could pray *with Him*.

It was good that I was exercising the power of prayer, "stirring myself up to take hold of Him," but I had forgotten what Isaiah said next. *"But now, O Lord, You are our Father; We are the clay, and You our potter; And all we are the work of Your hand..."*[24]

When Jesus walked the earth, He understood prayer better than anyone else ever has because He was intimately acquainted with the heart of the One He was praying to.

When we allow our perspective on intercession to be viewed through the lens of intimacy, we gain focus in releasing the throne room desires of God into the earth and into our lives. I believe that this is what it means to pray for His Kingdom to come and His will (the desires of His heart) to be done on earth as it is in heaven.

understanding the will of God

One of the most powerful indicators of the importance of intercession in the life of Jesus is His ongoing commitment to it. Even now, "He always lives to make intercession..."[25] That's astounding. As He is seated at the right hand of the Father, intercession flows out of Their time of being close together.

For Jesus, the understanding of the will of the Father was at the center of what He said, what He did, and what He prayed. When He said, "I only do what I see my Father doing," He was not setting a religious guideline for how we should pray for people. He was pointing to the communion that He shared with the One that He was one with. In

---

24   Isaiah. 64:8
25   Hebrews 7:25 Therefore He is also able to save to the uttermost those who come to God through Him, since He always lives to make intercession for them.

Romans 8, we get an even clearer picture of the intercession that takes place in the heavens. Paul tells us that both Jesus and the Holy Spirit are interceding on our behalf.

Who is he who condemns? It is Christ who died, and furthermore is also risen, who is even at the right hand of God, who also makes intercession for us. [26]

Likewise the Spirit also helps in our weaknesses. For we do not know what we should pray for as we ought, but the Spirit Himself makes intercession for us with groanings which cannot be uttered. [27]

In the presence of the Father, Jesus is interceding. "Likewise the Spirit" makes intercession for us. Intercession is a part of the culture of heaven. It is central to the community of the Trinity.

Paul gives us one more important detail about the intercession of heaven. In Romans 8:27, we see that the intercession that is taking place happens *according to the will of God.* [28]

What does the phrase 'according to the *will* of God' really mean? In general, I think many of us would say that God's will refers to something He wants. This is true in a broad sense, but if our intercession is informed only by the "broad will" of God, then we can miss the invitation to pray the prayers that He is praying *right now.*

For many of us, we pray according to the will of God like it was His last will and testament. *This is what He said should happen in His written record, so that is what I am going to pray.* Using God's Word to

---

26   Romans 8:34
27   Romans 8:26
28   Romans 8:27: Now He who searches the hearts knows what the mind of the Spirit is, because He makes intercession for the saints according to the will of God.

learn how to pray is so important, but we must remember that He is the Word and the Word is still alive. We come to understand God's will as we approach Him and see what He is actively, currently willing and wanting to happen.

praying from Daddy's lap

As we begin to grow in this "Invisible Lifestyle," we recognize that what started out as a desire to spend time *seeing the Father* (Intimacy), has turned into a time of seeing with the Father (Intercession). As I seek His face, He draws me into and invites me to share in His perspective. I am no longer left to pray about things according to the constrictions of this earth realm, but am now free to lean into what is on the heart of God. That is, after all, the core of what Jesus told His few when they asked Him to teach them how to pray.

But you, when you pray, go into your room, and when you have shut your door, pray to your Father who is in the secret place; and your Father who sees in secret will reward you openly. And when you pray, do not use vain repetitions as the heathen do. For they think that they will be heard for their many words.

Therefore do not be like them. For your Father knows the things you have need of before you ask Him. In this manner, therefore, pray: Our Father in heaven, hallowed be Your name. Your kingdom come. Your will be done on earth as it is in heaven.

Because of Jesus, I am welcomed into the secret place, the very throne room of God. In fact, I am seated with Him in heavenly places. [29]It is not a stretch to say that the best posture for my prayers is sitting in the lap of the Father. This reality drastically impacts the way I pray and intercede.

29   Ephesians 2:6: and raised us up together, and made us sit together in the heavenly places in Christ Jesus

It brings freedom to live and pray from heaven's perspective. From the earth realm, there can be so many things to overwhelm and weigh us down, but when I realize that I have been invited to gain the Father's perspective and pray in agreement with the prayers that are on His heart, what can overwhelm me? Listen to how Paul concludes his writing about Jesus interceding for us:

> It is *Christ who died, and furthermore is also risen, who is even at the right hand of God, who also makes intercession for us. Who shall separate us from the love of Christ? Shall tribulation, or distress, or persecution, or famine, or nakedness, or peril, or sword? It is written:*

> *"For Your sake we are killed all day long;*
> *We are accounted as sheep for the slaughter."*

> *Yet in all these things we are more than conquerors through Him who loved us. For I am persuaded that neither death nor life, nor angels nor principalities nor powers, nor things present nor things to come, nor height nor depth, nor any other created thing, shall be able to separate us from the love of God which is in Christ Jesus our Lord.*[30]

Paul directly connects the intercession that takes place at the throne of God with us no longer having to be overwhelmed. Nothing can separate us from His perfect love for us. His love makes us *more than conquerors*, and overcomers don't need to be overwhelmed.

As I think about being an overcomer, the lyrics to a song that my friend Jasmine wrote come to mind:

---

30   Romans 8:34-39

My Daddy's undefeated, unrelenting

He can't lose.

Your blood runs through my veins

So winning's what we do. [31]

Because I am seated together with Christ at the right hand of the Father, even my most feeble sounding prayers are prayed from the throne room, the place of victory. The fact that He has made me more than a conqueror means that I get to see things differently. Praying from this perspective not only changes the way we pray in overwhelming circumstances, but it also frees us up to pray for other people in a completely different way.

dirty prayers just won't do

Have you ever thought about the fact that you will never meet a person the Father has not been thinking about for eternity? Regardless of the person's situation, there is so much life in learning to pray for that person in view of the thoughts and desires the Father has for him or her. Humbly seeking the heart of God for someone honors our Heavenly Father and allows us access to a treasure trove of precious thoughts about the person for whom we are interceding.

How precious also are Your thoughts to me, O God!

How great is the sum of them!

If I should count them, they would be more in number than the sand;

When I awake, I am still with You. [32]

The thoughts of God towards us are countless, and they are all good ones. Whether I am praying for myself or for others, in this world there

31   From the song *Giants* by Jasmine Tate, 2014
32   Psalm 139:17-18

is plenty of dirt and decay to distract me from the treasure of what God is saying and thinking about a person—and it doesn't take much effort to find it. When we are honest, we are all aware of the dirt attached to our own lives. But what we all need is to intercede and be interceded for according to the treasure hidden beneath it.

> *It is the glory of God to conceal a matter,*
> *But the glory of kings is to search out a matter.*[33]

If my only option in prayer is to intercede from the perspective of the broken culture of this earth, then my prayers will focus on the dirt. But I am not limited to that perspective. I get to pray from the perspective of my seat in heaven. God knows about the dirt, but He is looking for those who will walk in the character of kings to search through and look past the dirt to discover the treasure.

One of the biggest hindrances that I have found in following Jesus in the area of intercession is that I don't always see people the way that God does. Jesus was sinless and selfless. That had to make praying for people a lot easier. To be honest, sometimes it is easy for me to have a bad attitude towards people who are in need of prayer. This is where coming into intercession as it is intertwined with intimacy can help me see things more clearly. It allows me to pray according to the rule and Ruler of heaven instead of the broken laws of the basic principles of this earth.[34]

In the C. S. Lewis classic, *The Lion, the Witch and the Wardrobe,* the White Witch comes to Aslan demanding that he turn Edmund over because he was a traitor. She said that all traitors belonged to her because of the 'Deep Magic,' which was the law on which Narnia was built. Aslan calls the witch into his quarters and then emerges to

---

33   Proverbs 25:2
34   Colossians 2:20

announce that the witch had renounced her claim on Edmund. The Great Lion, Aslan, then lays down his life as a sacrifice for 'the traitor' at the stone table.

Susan and Lucy witness the horror of the death of their King and stay with his body over night. Then at dawn, as they are finally preparing to leave him, the two girls hear the sound of the stone table breaking and witness Aslan famously resurrected back to life.

"Oh, Aslan!" cried both the children, staring up at him, almost as much frightened as they were glad..."But what does it all mean?" asked Susan when they were somewhat calmer.

"It means," said Aslan, "that though the Witch knew the Deep Magic, there is a magic deeper still which she did not know. Her knowledge goes back only to the dawn of time. But if she could have looked a little further back, into the stillness and the darkness before Time dawned, she would have read there a different incantation. She would have known that when a willing victim who had committed no treachery was killed in a traitor's stead, the Table would crack and Death itself would start working backward."[35]

For us today, there is a law of dirt and death in this earth. Just as Aslan is pictured having been there when the Deep Magic was written, Jesus was present at the creation. And while the enemy of our souls knew rightly that "the wages of sin is death,"[36] he missed an even greater truth—that before the foundations of the world, a Lamb had been chosen and slain.

---

35   Lewis C.S. (1950). *The Lion, the Witch and the Wardrobe*. Chapter 15. United Kingdom.
36   Romans 6:23

For if by the one man's offense death reigned through the one, much more those who receive abundance of grace and of the gift of righteousness will reign in life through the One, Jesus Christ.[37]

Because of Jesus, because of His love and redemption, we are free to live away from our destiny as dirt. And the price that set me free has been paid for every person on the planet. That means that we are no longer to be regarded as traitors, but as princes.

Now, as I intercede from the throne room to the King who sits on the throne, I have no need to look through my dirt at others, or to look at others' dirt. I can know and intercede for people according to the Spirit, according to the throne room desires of the King.

For the love of Christ compels us, because we judge thus: that if One died for all, then all died; and He died for all, that those who live should live no longer for themselves, but for Him who died for them and rose again.

Therefore, from now on, we regard no one according to the flesh. Even though we have known Christ according to the flesh, yet now we know Him thus no longer. Therefore, if anyone is in Christ, he is a new creation; old things have passed away; behold, all things have become new.[38]

intercession and the few

What does this view of intercession have to do with the culture of the few? I would submit that the prayer life of Jesus was the fuel for the culture He lived out with His disciples. That does not mean, however, that they just "got it." Not only did the masses misunderstand Him and the religious leaders persecute Him, but even His friends often missed out on the real meaning of the life Jesus was sharing with them.

37   Romans 5:17
38   2 Corinthians 5:14-17

Whether it was misunderstanding His teaching or not recognizing who He was, we know that the culture of the few around the life of Jesus was not without it's disappointing moments.

What was it like for Jesus to see Peter move from the revelation that Jesus was God's Son to missing out on God's plan for the cross and resurrection? How about for the King of glory to harness Himself to take on the form of a servant, only to have His disciples get into an argument over who would get to be the greatest in the Kingdom? Then there was that time when James and John were ready to call fire down and destroy towns full of people that Jesus was getting ready to die for. Or the night that the very core of Jesus' few couldn't stay awake with Him in the Garden of Gethsemane.

What was it like for Jesus to know that Peter would deny Him or that Thomas would doubt Him after He had suffered all things? And let's not forget that Judas, the one that betrayed Him, was one of His *closest friends*. One that Jesus had chosen because He wanted to.

It is easy for me to disconnect myself from Jesus in moments like these, because I know that I would fall short of His standard of loving these misfits. How did Jesus refuse to give up on a group of people who kept letting Him down? Let's reach out and grab that strand of DNA one more time:

Intimacy and Intercession. Seeing the Father. Seeing with Father.

On the disciples' best days, Jesus only does what He sees the Father do. In the midst of their most boneheaded moments, Jesus is still only doing what He sees the Father do. The Father still loved Peter during the denial, so Jesus kept loving Peter, too.

I can imagine Jesus seeking the face of the Father in such a disappointing moment, joining with One who would never disappoint Him. Father and Son begin to commune. The Father is vulnerable to the things that are on the Son's heart. The Son is vulnerable to things that are on the Father's heart.

I know these words are not recorded for us in Scripture, but I can just see Jesus looking up at the Father and shaking His head. *Did you hear what Peter just said? How long will I have to be with him for him to get why I am here?*

The Father smiles. *I know Son, but remember what I showed you about him. He is a rock, a keystone in the church that we are going to build into a bride for you.*

Yes, Jesus says. *Let your throne room desires come, your will be done on earth, in Peter's life, just like they are in heaven.*

Yes, the key to the invisible lifestyle of actively interceding for others out of intimacy is listening to the prayers that are on God's heart and agreeing with them. In the next chapter, we will take a more in depth look at how we can discern the things that are on God's heart to agree with Him in bringing His kingdom to earth.

13

shifting atmospheres

It was about one o'clock in the morning, and I was tired. We had just ended the first full day of a two-week missions school[39] that I was helping lead for college students from across the United States. I was ready for bed, but thought that it would be good to stop into the prayer room to see how it was taking shape.

The makeshift prayer room was nothing more than a dorm that had been set apart as a temporary sacred space for our stay on the campus of Haskell Indian Nations University in Lawrence, Kansas. Twenty-four hours earlier, a couple dozen students had been instructed to use a few art supplies and whatever they could find to create a place where they could meet with God. This would be a place for people to process and journal, a place where simple churches could practice learning to pray together.

Brown craft paper with prayers scribbled in sharpie lined the walls. Large index cards bearing prayer request were clothespinned to strings that had been thumbtacked to the corners of the back wall, creating visual depth and dimension. This is something God can work with, I thought.

---

39   tudent CPx / SCPX was started by Erik Fish in the summer of 2008 as an intensive missions training school focused on disciple-making and church planting.

As I walked through the prayer room, glancing at the artwork and reading the simple but passionate prayers of the students, I had no idea that something life-changing was about to happen. I finished reading the last prayer hanging on the clothesline and then went to investigate a noise I'd heard from inside of a little room that had been built by draping a sheet around some stacked furniture in the corner.

I walked over and quietly pulled back the sheet to see what was happening in this prayer closet within the prayer room. Two mattresses lay on the floor behind the sheet. There, half sitting, half lying on the beds was Alex, one of the students from Arizona.

He had fallen asleep with his journal and was somewhat startled to wake up and see me standing over him. I remember the slightly embarrassed smile that filled His face. His smile made my heart glad that I had stumbled upon his sleepy attempt to process what God was doing.

I remember stepping back from the curtain sensing a connection with Alex. Ironically, our initial late night encounter repeated itself at least two more times before the training was over. Each time, there were few words spoken, but the connection between us grew. There was a certain knowing that was taking place between us. I could easily relate to the heart of this young man who was just trying to spend some extra time with God.

On one of those nights, I remember walking out of the prayer room praying. With a smile still on my face, I began to ask God what He had to say about Alex. Immediately I was struck by the pleasure of God the Father over him. I sensed God speaking to my heart about Alex's identity and the need for him to grow in confidence and in his ability to be himself.

As the mission school came to a close, I talked with Alex about some of the things God had been showing me. I was excited when I saw Alex's name on the list of a few students I was to call and check in on once or twice a month. I remember hoping that the connection would grow, but I had no idea that years later, this Filipino student from Arizona would uproot his life to move across the country to follow Jesus with our family and the church community that we had planted in Pennsylvania.

While I had no idea, I cannot say that I was completely surprised. Even though our initial meetings seemed to be based on me interrupting his accidental sleep in the prayer room, God had been building something more from the very beginning.

It was not compelling conversations that endeared Alex to my wife and I, but the invisible connection that came from discerning the Father's heart for this incredible young man. In *seeing with the Father*, we knew that anything we could do to love and encourage Alex would be a worthwhile investment in the Kingdom. Now, he is one of the "few" that we have committed to disciple, and we are so honored to share life with him.

people, places, and things

The story about Alex is important because it illustrates the value of gaining God's heart for people in the midst of building Kingdom connections. This is a key in growing in a lifestyle of prayer and intercession. There are many that have written about other important aspects of intercession, but I cannot get away from how important seeking the face of the Father has been in my own life.

Remember that Jesus did not live by a script; He lived out of the closeness of His relationship with His Father, allowing His actions, words and prayers to be based on what He saw the Father doing. It is impossible for us to truly follow Jesus until we are more committed to doing what we see the Father doing than we are to the script that we would write for our own lives.

Embracing this life means that we might not get advance warning about the pivotal moments that God is orchestrating in and around us. God could have told me before I walked into the prayer room that first night, *I am going to connect you to a young man from Arizona who will be sleeping in the prayer room tonight,* but He did not. There was no prophetic word, just an opportunity for me to try to see what the Father was doing as life happened.

Father, what do you have to say about Alex?

I do not want to pretend that I have mastered seeing with the Father. There are too many times that I go through life absorbed in my own dirt to think about what is going on in God's heart. No, I have not mastered this, but one thing that I have learned over the past several years is that the Father wants to speak to me, and He really likes it when I ask Him what is on His heart.

In this chapter, we will look at how we can lean into God's heart to learn how to intercede for the people, places and things that we find there. Again, this is connected to the idea of allowing our prayer and intercession to flow out of close relationship with God. Jesus said that He wanted to transition His few from a place of servanthood to friendship. This would be evidenced to them by the fact that He was going to let them know whatever the Father was doing.[40]

---

40   John 15:15

God wants to speak to us about individuals and families, college campuses and cities, neighborhoods and nations. He wants to show us what is happening and what He wants to happen. He is looking for sons and daughters who will take an interest in the world's people and their problems and lean into what is in His heart for a solution.

i was hoping you would ask

Several years ago, my friend Jessie—who was co-leading our summer internship at the time—was working with our students on learning how to hear the voice of God. She had done the core of the teaching several days earlier, and on this particular afternoon, it was time to practice. Thirteen of us crammed into the small living room of our training house as Jessie began to speak.

Ok. Let's practice hearing God's voice. Today we are going to ask God...

This was not uncommon for Jessie. She is really gifted at helping people recognize that our God is the God who speaks. From Genesis to Revelation, the Scriptures reveal the story of a God who loves to relate to those He made in His own image. One of Jessie's favorite ways to equip people is to have them ask God questions. Often times they are questions like, "God, what do you have to say about me?" or "God, remind me of one of your favorite moments from my childhood."

As we sat in the living room that day, these were the kinds of questions we were prepared to answer. But this time, Jessie went a very different direction.

Today we are going to ask God what is on His heart for our neighbor, Tim.

You could have heard a pin drop in the room as people opened their journals and began to wait on the Lord. After a few minutes, I began to hear sniffling and muffled tears.

You see, Tim was not 'one of us.' *Our Summer in the Grove*⁴¹ crew was made up of bright, young leaders who were all in their early twenties. Tim was twice the age of our interns, and life had not been kind to him. His heart had been broken by a failed marriage and though he had tried, he had never really found a healthy way to deal with that pain.

Tim had a reputation around town as someone to stay away from. It seemed that most people didn't know how to relate to him, which left him to live a pretty lonely life. He wanted to be known but did not know how to do that.

Several of our girls felt uncomfortable with any level of interaction with him. This created a tension anytime we talked about trying to be intentional about building relationships with our neighbors. And this is where Jessie went with our journaling question for the day.

After ten minutes or so, Jessie looked at one of the students and asked him if God had spoken anything to him.

Yes, God said He had been waiting for us to ask Him about Tim.

I was undone. I sat there and listened and watched as the atmosphere of the room was transformed. Around the circle we went, listening to the things that God—the One who had created Tim with the purpose of knowing and loving him—had to say to us. By the time we had gone around the entire circle, everyone was ready to pray.

---

41   Summer in the Grove is a 12-week internship that focuses on spiritual formation, disciple making and leadership development. It is a part of AOX, the church community where Brad and Adriane serve as leaders.

We started with a healthy dose of repentance for our ungodly attitudes about this precious man that God loved. We then moved into intercession for Tim, praying the prayers that were on God's heart. It was one of the most powerful prayer times I have ever been a part of; and not just because of the power of our prayers to change Tim's heart, but because of the power of God's prayers to change ours.

Our interns began looking for opportunities to build friendships with Tim. It was less than a month later that he gave his heart to Jesus and was baptized by one of the students. By the time we were preparing for the next Summer in the Grove, Tim was hosting a simple church at his house.

discerning atmospheres

Spiritual gifts have, sadly, been a place of much controversy in the church. There has been much debate about how to use them, who can use them, and which gifts are still supposed to be used today. The purpose of this book is not to talk about spiritual gifts, but it is impossible for me to encourage readers who are interested in seeing cultural transformation to look at and follow the life of Jesus without acknowledging that this is an impossible lifestyle. It is a lifestyle that only becomes possible as I humble myself and learn to walk with the Person of the Holy Spirit, the One that Jesus promised He would send to be our Helper.[42]

I remember being struck by my need to learn how to co-operate with Holy Spirit as I listened to the thoughts that a leader from a historically conservative movement was sharing at an ordination service I was attending. This man was the bishop that oversaw all of the churches for his denomination in North America. As he stood to speak to the large crowd, he began to talk about how he had been recognizing how preposterous it was to allow the misuse of certain gifts by some people to discourage us from using good gifts that a good God had left for us.

42   John 14:15-18

"How can we look at God and tell Him that we don't need the gifts that He left us to build up the body—and then turn around and ask Him how to build up the body?"

This was such great insight. I became even more resolved to hunger for and desire everything that God had for me in terms of spiritual gifts. We should never be afraid to *earnestly desire*[43] spiritual gifts when we are in pursuit of bringing the Love of heaven to earth. Every good gift comes from a loving Father who releases those gifts for the purpose of loving and building up the body, making us more ready to share the message of Love with those who do not know Him.[44]

One of the gifts that the New Testament offers as relevant to a life-style of intercession is discernment. I want to be clear that when I speak about leaning into God's heart to see what He has to say about an individual, a place, or a situation, I am not saying that you should expect to hear an audible voice from heaven in response. While some people might experience this, most often the Lord will respond to us through the use of one of the gifts that are listed in the Scriptures to the church.

Most of the people that I know who practice *seeing with the Father* are actually operating in the spiritual gift of discernment, though it is definitely possible for God to use other means to convey the things of His heart. He is God, after all. He can do whatever He is willing to do.

But when I speak of the spiritual gift of discernment, I am talking becoming spiritually aware of something because the Spirit of God is making me aware of it or is bringing something specific to my memory. When I spiritually discern what is happening in a person or a situation, it is different than coming to a conclusion based on my natural observations. It is a grace from God, a gift from a Holy, loving Father that wants to build me up and build up those around me.

---

43   1 Corinthians 13:1
44   James 1:17

When Jessie asked our interns to ask God what He had to say about Tim, we began to intentionally take time to discern what was already on God's heart. Discernment is a revelatory gift, meaning that the Spirit of God uses it to reveal what is already there.

His heart towards Tim was always for Tim to know Him and experience love. God's attitude towards Tim did not change when we began to ask Him what was on His heart. Ours did.

When we take time to regularly discern the heart of God for people, places, and things, we will regularly experience a shifting in the atmospheres of that for which we are praying. I believe that nations, regions, cities, neighborhoods, families and people all have distinct spiritual identities. They have cultures, climates, and atmospheres. As sons and daughters of God, who have been given authority on this earth, we have a say in what those cultures, climates, and atmospheres look like.

You can see this as you walk the streets of your hometown. I encourage you to begin to intentionally practice seeing with the Father as you spend time in your neighborhood or at your favorite park. Begin to ask Him to show you what is currently happening in those places and then ask Him what is on His heart?

I once heard a wise, experienced teacher illustrate this point as he stood in front of a large church in the Midwest. He asked the audience, "What thoughts pop into your mind when I say Las Vegas?" Immediately you could feel a spiritual discomfort in the room. It was easily discernible that many people had negative thoughts or emotions attached to 'Sin City.'

"What about San Francisco?" he said. Again, you could see that there were associations that many of us made with San Francisco that carried a negative connotation.

What would happen if we began to ask God what was on His heart for these cities? Instead of allowing sin and brokenness to create the identity of cities that are full of people that Jesus died for, why don't we seek the heart of the Father for what He has to say about them?

Jesus spoke to cities. Yes, He spoke to the crowds that gathered in a city—but He went beyond that. He spoke to the collective spiritual identity of places.

O Jerusalem, Jerusalem, the one who kills the prophets and stones those who are sent to her! How often I wanted to gather your children together, as a hen gathers her chicks under her wings, but you were not willing! See! Your house is left to you desolate; for I say to you, you shall see Me no more till you say, 'Blessed is He who comes in the name of the Lord!' [45]

Woe to you, Chorazin! Woe to you, Bethsaida! For if the mighty works which were done in you had been done in Tyre and Sidon, they would have repented long ago in sackcloth and ashes. [46]

Even though there were people present as Jesus spoke, we find Him addressing the cities themselves. I believe He was speaking to the collective spiritual identity of these cities about the spiritual cultures, climates and atmospheres that they possessed. This concept may seem foreign to some, but it is actually talked about quite frequently in the gospels.

---

45   Matthew 23:37-39
46   Matthew 11:21

In addition to the three cities listed in the Scriptures above, we see Jesus speaking similarly of Capernaum.[47] Then there is also His interaction with the people of Nazareth, where *He did not do many mighty works there because of their unbelief.*[48] It appears from the reading of that passage that there was an atmosphere of unbelief that impacted all who gathered at the synagogue to hear Jesus.

shifting...

Learning to shift spiritual atmospheres is an integral part of cultural transformation. As we follow Jesus—cultivating deep, discipleship relationships with a handful of people—we need to become confident in the heart of God to pour out His love and power on the people, places, and things that He will lead us to encounter. We also need to be confident in the ability of the Spirit of God that dwells within us to bring about the changes that He wants to bring—understanding that it is *Christ in us, that is the hope of glory.*[49]

Following Jesus with the concepts and goals of *Culture of the Few* in mind, we can intentionally cultivate a culture of intercession that is informed by the heart of God in the lives of those we are discipling. We remain capable of walking through hard times with our few because we have accessed the Father's heart for them—and then we teach them how to do that for others as well.

This results in being able to develop a community of people who are praying in agreement for people, places, and things from heaven's perspective. There is so much power in agreement. This is how I have seen atmospheres shift in the places that we live life. I seek the face of the Father to see the Father. He invites me to intercede for others as I see with the Father. I agree with God about the prayers that are on His heart. I agree with others who are seeking the face of the Father and who are interested in the prayers that are on His heart.

47   Matthew 11:23
48   Matthew 13:58
49   Colossians 1:27

The key in this type of lifestyle is to keep our eyes on the Father, not allowing what we are seeing in the natural world to trump what we are seeing from our throne room position on Daddy's lap. It is important to remember that God is looking for those to whom He has delegated authority on the earth to come together in agreement with Him.

So I sought for a man among them who would make a wall, and stand in the gap before Me on behalf of the land, that I should not destroy it; but I found no one.[50]

When the prophet Ezekiel recorded these words, God's people were living under the old covenant. I believe that we live under a better covenant because of the cross, where Jesus took all of the wrath and indignation of God against sin. It would be a sad mistake to believe that God wanted to destroy any city or land, even under the old covenant. In this verse, He is clearly looking for someone to make a stand in intercession.

So what do we who live under the new covenant do with Scriptures like this? I think it would be foolish to dismiss the work of Christ on the cross, where the judgment of God was poured out on our sin and replaced with Christ's right standing so that we could be restored to the Father. But it would be equally foolish to ignore the spiritual law of sowing and reaping that God established as a part of creation. While the wrath of God has been satisfied, there are still consequences—for better or worse—for the way that we live life.

Jesus knew that He had come to satisfy the justice of God for sin. He preached a message that invited individuals to come to Him so He could reconcile them to the Father. Still, He pleaded with, wept over, and rebuked cities because He knew that there were consequences for the collective rejection of His message; that while there would be

50   Ezekiel 22:30

individuals who would find Him in the midst of the crowds, the atmosphere over the cities would serve the purpose of the enemy to put blinders on the masses.

While this book is not concerned with a theological treatise of how the judgment of God works, we can draw an invaluable conclusion from Jesus' attitude towards cities in our development of understanding the culture of the few: The church has both a huge opportunity and a sacred responsibility to intercede. Through informed intercession, we can shift atmospheres over our neighborhoods, cities, regions, and nations. This is the heart of God.

The heart of God has always been love. It is true that we have a greater revelation of that love through the person of Jesus Christ under the new covenant, but even in the days of the Old Testament, God's heart was still mercy. Consider the story of the destruction of Sodom and Gomorrah. God's heart was to talk with His friend Abraham about what was happening. He was vulnerable to the pleadings and cries of Abraham for mercy.

Then the men rose from there and looked toward Sodom, and Abraham went with them to send them on the way. And the Lord said, "Shall I hide from Abraham what I am doing, since Abraham shall surely become a great and mighty nation, and all the nations of the earth shall be blessed in him? For I have known him, in order that he may command his children and his household after him, that they keep the way of the Lord, to do righteousness and justice, that the Lord may bring to Abraham what He has spoken to him.[51]

It was out of friendship that God decided to let Abraham know what was happening down there. I can almost hear Him thinking, *I know that he will care. I know he will intercede.*

---

51   Genesis 18:19

And the Lord said, "Because the outcry against Sodom and Gomorrah is great, and because their sin is very grave, I will go down now and see whether they have done altogether according to the outcry against it that has come to Me; and if not, I will know.[52]

Because of the wickedness of the city, a sound had been released in the heavens. This outcry demanded a response from God, but the heart of God was to share this with His friend and intercessor first. We know the story of how Abraham pleaded with God. There was a search for righteous men in the city.

God, please don't be angry, but would you spare the city for fifty, for forty, thirty, twenty, for ten righteous men?

The "yes" that was in God's heart shows His nature. He is just. He is kind. He is vulnerable to the pleadings of those who will intercede.

the sound in the heavens

As we know, there were not ten righteous men found in the city. Tragically, Sodom's rejection of the Creator led to its destruction. For the purpose of understanding our roles as intercessors, let's look again at what drew the attention of God to Sodom and Gomorrah.

I will go down now and see whether they have done altogether according to the outcry against it that has come to Me; and if not, I will know.

There is a sound released in the heavens based on the activity of the earth. This sound could be positive or negative, beckoning blessing or bringing correction. The key in this story is that God was responding to the sound. In the case of Sodom and Gomorrah, the cry was against the cities. Let's look at the story of Cornelius to see what it looks like for God to respond according to a sound on behalf of a people.

There was a certain man in Caesarea called Cornelius, a centurion of what was called the Italian Regiment, a devout man and one who feared God with all his household, who gave alms generously to the people, and prayed to God always. About the ninth hour of the day he saw clearly in a vision an angel of God coming in and saying to him, "Cornelius!" And when he observed him, he was afraid, and said, "What is it, lord?"

So he said to him, "Your prayers and your alms have come up for a memorial before God.[53]

This is an intriguing story about God responding to the sound that had come to him through the life of a man who had not yet been born again. God is releasing angelic visitations in response to the prayers and generosity of an unsaved man.

Not only did He send an angel to Cornelius, but He also draws Peter into a trance and changes the rules of engagement for the gospel going out to the gentiles forever. Why? Because of *the memorial* that had risen up before Him, because of the sound of a man who hadn't even heard the gospel yet.

This story is significant in terms of intercession and the conversation of shifting atmospheres because it paints an accurate picture of the posture of heavens' vulnerability to the prayers and righteous living of those who fear God on the earth. I believe that if we hold the story of Cornelius in tension with the story of Sodom and Gomorrah, we can see that there is a sound rising from the earth realm into the heavens. What exactly that sound is varies by household, neighborhood, city,

---

53   Acts 10:1-4

and nation, but as the church, we have something to say about it. Even if the sound that rises over our city or nation is coming against it, we have an opportunity and responsibility to shift the atmosphere through intercession.

come into the light

I want to conclude this chapter with a story about what it looks like to discern atmospheres and release the Kingdom of God. Some of you may have noticed that there are two stories in this book about Sean. One is about a messy disciple who was unashamed to share his testimony. The other was about me praying for someone who had not yet come to Jesus. As you probably have concluded by the last few sentences, these stories are both about the same person.

I would like to tell you the "in-between" part of this story to connect the dots. About six months after my encounter with God in the "school of prayer" at the back of the conference sanctuary, we decided to have a special weekend of prayer. We had gathered with friends from around our town to pray and worship for seventy-two hours, rotating shifts to seek the face of God while declaring His promises over our city. The specific focus of this '72 HOP' was praying for a soul harvest during a large arts and music festival that was held in our city every summer.

During the last leg of the weekend, we asked everyone who had covered a shift to come back and join together in one last time of intercession for our lost friends. We went around the room praying for people by name, calling them to come to Jesus, speaking to their spirit man to come into the light of a life in Christ.

At this point, we had no idea where Sean was. It had been several months since he had left our house and moved out of state to live with an aunt. He would check in with us occasionally, but we had not heard from him in weeks. That night, I became so burdened for Sean that my heart hurt. We had known him for a few years by that point, but it seemed like we had been praying for him to come to Jesus forever.

We had no idea that Sean had been locked up in jail for several weeks. The police had picked him up for petty theft while he was trying to find food for his family. As we were praying, Sean was sitting in his cell, contemplating where his life was headed.

Sean had been around us enough to know what we believed about prayer, but as a practicing pagan, he had been clear that his "prayer life" was quite different. Instead of praying to the Father of Lights, his prayers often relied on the power of darkness.

That night, as we joined in with the prayers of the Father, inviting our friend to 'Come into the light,' Sean began to turn his heart to God.

"God, if you are there and if you care, please help me," he prayed. "Please get me out of here."

Sean had no money for bail and no ability to do anything to change his circumstances. Yet within a few hours of his prayer, the officer in charge of him came to him and said, "I have no idea why I am doing this, but I am going to let you go."

Without knowing that we had been praying for him, Sean made a beeline back to Ellwood City as soon as he was released. Within forty-eight hours of our prayer time, Sean had been released from jail and was back in town for the festival about which we'd been praying.

My face exploded into a huge smile when I saw him. I could feel the anticipation of what was coming. Within just a few days, I received a call from my friend Chuck.

"I am here with Sean, and he has something he wants to tell you," Chuck said.

Tears of joy began to flow down my face before Sean even got on the phone.

"I know that it's taken a long time," Sean started. "But I wanted you to know that I just said 'Yes' to Jesus."

A few days later, we were able to get together and hear about his experience praying in jail, and how he was released just hours later. Sean was dumbstruck that we had been praying for him at the same time. How could we have known to be praying for him at that exact moment?

The truth is that we didn't know we needed to pray for Sean any more on that night than we had the previous two years—but the Father did. No one in our prayer circle had received a prophetic word that Sean was in jail or a revelation that this was a pivotal moment in his life. We had simply spent time seeking the Father, and despite our ignorance to Sean's situation, the Father had invited us to see with Him. Our intercession had been informed not by the greatness of our giftings, but by the perfect love of the Heavenly Father's heart.

As we make the Father's face our focus and lean into His perfect love as the fuel for our intercession, we will undoubtably witness the power of heaven shifting things around us. More importantly, we will recognize that the atmosphere of our own hearts will change. The joy of engaging the heart of God from a place of rest and trust, will free us to pray bold prayers that move heaven and change the world.

14

living inside the answer

As we embrace the invisible lifestyle of intercession and experience the shift in the atmosphere of our own hearts, as well as in the people, places and things around us, it is important that we keep our eyes focused on the life of Jesus. Again, He is the One we are following, the ultimate Agent of Change. As we wrap up this section on *Intercession*, I want to look at a few key truths that Jesus taught His disciples and modeled for them.

The first of these keys is persistence. I admit that the need for persistence in prayer has often baffled me. After all, we pray to an all-knowing, all-powerful God. Why would we need to pray more than once about something? While some have suggested that continuing to pray about a matter demonstrates a lack of faith, Jesus teaches His friends the importance of continued prayer on several occasions.

In Luke 18, Jesus shares a parable about a persistent widow and an unjust judge. It is clear from the story that the judge had no fear of God and no regard for man. Yet because the widow continued to bring her case before the judge, he acted on her behalf.

I have always been curious about this parable. Why would Jesus draw a parallel between a loving Father and this unjust judge. Let's look at the introduction to the story to find the answer.

Then He spoke a parable to them, that men always ought to pray and not lose heart, saying: "There was in a certain city a judge who did not fear God nor regard man." [54]

I believe that the instruction that accompanies this parable gives us insight into how important perseverance in prayer really is. *Men ought always to pray and not lose heart.* While we pray to a Father who loves us perfectly, in this parable of a desperate woman who relentlessly makes her request know to a man who didn't care, Jesus is painting a picture for His followers that persistence over time is essential in prayer.

This wasn't the first time that Jesus instructed His few about the importance of persisting prayer. In fact, it was a direct part of His answer when the disciples asked Him to teach them how to pray. In Luke 11, just after the *Lord's Prayer*, Jesus tells another story. This time it is about a "friend" going to his neighbor at midnight to get some bread for an unexpected house guest.

Initially, the neighbor refuses the request, explaining that it is too late and that he is already in bed. But the friend *keeps knocking.* Once again, we see that the request was answered because of perseverance.

I say to you, though he will not rise and give to him because he is his friend, yet because of his persistence he will rise and give him as many as he needs. [55]

---

54   Luke 18:1-2
55   Luke 11:8

In this passage, Jesus goes on to instruct His friends to ask, seek and knock. In context, He is really saying to keep asking, keep seeking and keep knocking. He closes that passage assuring the disciples of the heart of the One they are praying to.

If you then, being evil, know how to give good gifts to your children, how much more will your heavenly Father give the Holy Spirit to those who ask Him![56]

We pray to a trustworthy, all-powerful, all-knowing God whose heart is to invite us into seeing His Kingdom come on the earth. So why do we have to keep praying? There is something about spending time with God, focusing on His face and praying the prayers that are on His heart that makes us ready for the answers that we are praying for.

It is easy for world-changers to pray big prayers before we are ready to live out the answers. I will often ask young adults if they are glad that God didn't answer the first time they asked Him to give them a spouse. Usually, people begin to laugh and shake their heads when they realize how catastrophic it would have been had God granted their first request.

I must admit that there are times when I am stirred to pray mighty prayers, but lose passion or interest over time. Sometimes God answers prayers that I had forgotten I had even prayed. It's easier to ask for the nations than it is to disciple them. It is right to ask God for the nations, but persistence in prayer is a part of God building you to a place where you can steward the answer. I believe that is the heart of why we are called to pray without ceasing.

stewarding the future

As Jesus taught about the importance of persistence in prayer, it is important to remember that He was speaking these words to the ones He would leave to turn the world upside down. While there was value in what He was teaching them in the moment, I believe He was building them towards their future. He was speaking to those who would lose their lives to see the "foolish" message of the gospel spread. His friends, who would pay a high price to follow Him, would need the steadfastness that is produced through a life of persevering prayer.

This connects us to the next prayer key that I want to highlight from the life Jesus. Prayer makes us ready for our future in Him. In John 17, we see perhaps the best expression of the future focus of the intercession of Jesus. Just before He is betrayed, Jesus takes time to be with the Father. He prays for Himself, but quickly turns His attention to His followers. He prays for what life will be like for them after He is gone. These were not nameless, faceless people. These were the ones that He had given Himself to for three years.

Jesus didn't stop with His few, but He looked past the present into the lives of those who would come after He had returned to the Father.

I do not pray for these alone, but also for those who will believe in Me through their word; that they all may be one, as You, Father, are in Me, and I in You; that they also may be one in Us, that the world may believe that You sent Me.[57]

As Jesus interceded on the night He was betrayed, we were on His heart and mind. Just before He paid the price for our salvation, He joins Himself with the Father's heart for future generations. As Jesus was preparing to lay down His life, He prays a prayer that is still being answered today.

---

57   John 17:20-21

In reading John 17, I am struck by how the cry of Jesus' prayer is for His followers, and that the Father might be glorified. Jesus is the central figure to the whole gospel story, yet He models a confident humility in prayer. Knowing that the hope of mankind's past, present, and future rests on His shoulders, His intercession was not focused on Himself.

It is worth mentioning that as we follow Jesus into intercession, we must follow Him in humility. As we learn to steward the future through prayer, we can be tempted to begin to take credit for what God is doing. It is easy to allow self-importance to grow in our hearts, and answered prayers to become our identity.

Real stewardship requires enough ownership that we are responsible to persist in our prayers until they are answered. But we do this remembering that it is an honor to join with our Father in seeing His throne room desires poured out on the earth. It is essential to follow Jesus in focusing our prayers on others while giving all of the glory to God.

a holy experiment

As I look at the life of Jesus, I am astounded by the record of how much time He spent praying. The last prayer key that I want to bring to your attention is simply remembering the significance of prayer itself. We have already mentioned that Jesus taking time to pray is one of the most consistent, easily recognizable habits or patterns of His life.

It frustrates me how often I can forget about the significance of prayer. It is not that I forget to pray, but that sometimes it is easy for me to think that my prayers are insignificant. I have seen God do so many amazing things, yet still it is easy for me to think that my prayers are too small to make a difference in a big situation. Then, when we ask God for His heart for people, places, and things, it can feel like we are in way over our heads.

There have been many times in my life that I have prayed prayers that seem ridiculous. There have been moments when I have met in a room with just a handful of people seeking the Lord on behalf of a nation that is undergoing political upheaval, a natural disaster, or some other great tragedy. In those moments, I hear a quiet whisper mocking me, telling me that there is nothing that our little prayers can do in such a big situation. There are times in which prayer can feel more like a pipe dream, when the things that I pray for seem so far away. But I pray to the One who says, *"Call on me, and I will answer you. I will show you great and mighty things you do not know."*[58]

I experienced this recently when I was leading a prayer time with about fifteen others at our church in Grove City. On this particular night, we were praying for the city of Pittsburgh and for the gospel to spread through Asia. Sometimes, our prayer times can feel especially alive and inspiring. In those times there is almost a buzz of expectation as we pray and discern together. But on this night, our gathering didn't feel too alive or inspired.

I sat up front and looked around, thinking about the ridiculousness of our little group praying for the city of Pittsburgh. Who did we think we were? The thought seemed even more preposterous as we prayed for the *Back to Jerusalem Movement*, and for the gospel to impact millions along the silk road.

What could the uninspired prayers of a handful of us really do?

Of course, I know that *where two or three are gathered,*[59] God is present and ready to answer, but my heart was still overwhelmed by the size of the thing we were praying for that night. As I sat there feeling

58   Jeremiah 33:3
59   Matthew 18:20

sorry for myself, the Holy Spirit reminded me of the incredible story of William Penn. I wasn't quite sure where He was going, but what I learned that night shifted my perspective on prayer in a way that I will never forget.

Before my move from North Carolina all I really knew about William Penn was that he founded the state of Pennsylvania and that many people thought he was the guy on the Quaker oatmeal box. Upon moving to the state that Penn founded, I became aware of some of the spiritual history that led to him leaving his native England to engage in what he called "a holy experiment."

William Penn had grown up in a turbulent time in the history of England. His father was an admiral in the the King of England's Navy and had helped restore the monarchy after the English Civil War. This triumph made the Penn family a prominent one. Admiral Penn had high hopes for his son William. He sent him away to school to grow his education and to hopefully become a respectable citizen of the King. During William Penn's time away, he encountered an expression of Christianity unlike anything he'd experienced from the Church of England or the Roman Catholic church it had broken away from. Penn was exposed to a movement that would be called the Quakers, who in large part rejected the way that the Church of England was operating.

In the Quakers' eyes, the Church of England had changed their hierarchical titles, but kept much of the structure of the Church of Rome. This change may have had a different appearance, but still carried much of the same religious substance. The Quakers longed for a simpler, more authentic expression of a life following Jesus. William Penn left the Church of England to join this new movement, and this caused him big problems with his father and with the King. After all, here was the son of the Admiral who had helped restore the King to his throne, defying the church that the King led.

William Penn's fascination with and commitment to the Quaker movement led to the forming of a strong relationship with George Fox—the primary leader of the Quakers. Penn soon began to write the stories and theological thoughts of George Fox, and in fact became one of the Quakers' most influential theologians himself. Penn went on to be imprisoned for preaching the gospel because his ideas did not fall under the guidelines of the Church of England. At one point, William Penn even left England and settled in County Cork, Ireland in an attempt to allow his tempestuous relationship with his father and the King to cool down and to watch over his father's holdings there.

While in Ireland, Penn continued to attend Quaker meetings in Cork. It was there that he reconnected with Thomas Loe, who had been an early influence in his spiritual journey. Again, Penn was arrested for attending the Quaker meetings. It was during this season of his life that he began to articulate why he was attracted to the Quakers' way of following Jesus and the Scriptures. Penn believed that the Quakers had no political agenda and that they should be free from the laws that were designed to limit political minorities from spreading their propaganda. He saw the way the King created laws that affected the spread of the gospel of Jesus as religious persecution. This perspective began to shape the prayers and dreams in his heart that would later be expressed in forming Pennsylvania.

Once Penn had been released from jail, he was recalled to London by his father. Upon his return, Penn found himself in trouble once again because of his faith. Still in his early twenties, William Penn's strained relationship with his father and with the crown left him homeless and with no inheritance. Despite his hardships, Penn grew in his passion for Jesus, for righteousness and for justice. His service to the Quaker church led him to travel throughout Europe. He spent much of his time in Germany, witnessing the hardships of religious exiles who were a part of the Protestant movement. There, he also saw the trials that German Catholics went through as the religious tides of the Reformation in that country began to turn.

Through all of Penn's journey a longing was forming in his heart. Penn believed that the Bible that he read, and the Jesus that he followed, offered hope and a real sense of justice for all people. Penn dreamed and prayed for a society that would be governed by men who would willingly place themselves under the teachings of Scripture. He famously said, "If we will not be governed by God we will be ruled by tyrants."

This set of beliefs was at odds with the King and the Church of England. Eventually, Penn was imprisoned in the Tower of London because of his faith. He had been charged with both heresy and treason by the crown. During this time his father became seriously ill. While his father did not agree with his son's convictions or conclusions, he grew to admire William's sense of integrity and willingness to sacrifice for what he believed. Against William Penn's wishes, Admiral Penn paid the fines to see his son released from prison. He also reinstated his son's inheritance and appealed to the King to offer his son protection in exchange for the Admiral's lifetime of service to the crown.

When his father died, William Penn found himself a wealthy man. It did not change his approach to life, however, and because of that he found himself imprisoned once again. Upon release, Penn returned to his missionary work in Holland and Germany before making a request to the King for land in the New World. This land would be used as a home for Quakers and others suffering religious persecution under authorities of England and Rome. In this request, Penn was making an appeal based on the stirring of his heart, that "there might be room for such a holy experiment."

Penn had suffered a loss of finances, social status, political opportunity, and had been imprisoned multiple times for his faith; throughout the process, however, the burning desire to see a new expression of government released upon the earth continued to grow. In making his request to the King, he was asking the Crown, which had been his enemy, to grant to him the proprietorship of a new colony. This request gave the King the opportunity to repay the debt of gratitude that he owed to Penn's father and to rid himself of the agitation that Penn and the other Quakers had been causing him once and for all.

So, the King granted his request. In fact, William Penn became the recipient of the largest land-grant ever given to an individual in the colonies. And that piece of the New World that would become Pennsylvania was founded with this prayer: "That there may be room for such a holy experiment. For the nations want a precedent, and my God will make it the seed of the nation."

William Penn began to lay out the groundwork of his "holy experiment." He was heavily involved in the planning of Philadelphia, which would serve as the capital of his new colony. Through the study of his Christian beliefs, research, and prayer, Penn began to lay the framework of a system of government that would be based on checks and balances and the separation of powers. This new government would have three branches. The executive branch, in which he acted as royal governor, was held in check by a legislative branch that represented the people. Both of these branches would work together with the judicial branch. This was significantly different from how the courts of England operated. Little did William Penn know that his new experiment would serve as the laboratory of a new nation. In fact, some historians called William Penn "the Grandfather of Independence."

putting the pieces together

Just a little over five years ago, my family and I found ourselves at the Pennsylvania State Capitol in Harrisburg. This is right around the time that we were in the process of planting the church we now lead in Grove City. As we spent time praying about forming this new community of faith, the word "experiment" continued to surface in my heart. At first, I did not know why this word seemed so strongly connected to what God had called us to do here. To be honest, I was very uncomfortable at the thought of communicating anything that seemed experimental, because it seemed unsafe.

During that visit to the state capitol, I remembered William Penn's prayer that Pennsylvania would become a "holy experiment." As I walked into the capitol building I looked up and saw the words to Penn's prayer engraved in the rotunda. I began to weep almost uncontrollably at the thought that although I was following Jesus and not William Penn, I found myself living inside the answer of someone else's prayer. The things that seemed most important to those who were forming our new church community seemed intimately connected to the prayers and dreams that had led William Penn through his long and hard journey to form Pennsylvania. Even at it's most basic level, God could never have called us here if "here" didn't exist.

I don't know where Penn was when he first began to pray in the late 1600's for "room for such a holy experiment." Maybe he was in his father's home in County Cork, or maybe it was when he was imprisoned in the Tower of London—it doesn't really matter. Today, I live in the answer to that prayer. I pray that God would give us the courage and conviction to pray prayers that future generations can live in.

I see this in the life of Jesus and the prayer from John 17. As He was praying for those who would believe because of the words of His few, He was partnering with God in creating a future that we are living in today. His prayer for us was that we would know His glory and be one with Him.

And the glory which You gave Me I have given them, that they may be one just as We are one: I in them, and You in Me; that they may be made perfect in one, and that the world may know that You have sent Me, and have loved them as You have loved Me.[60]

This is an astounding prayer! In fact, it would be too good to be true if Jesus, Himself, didn't pray it. But He did pray it. It reflects the heart of the Father and creates a beautiful invitation for us to live inside of. Living inside the answer of Jesus' prayer will lead us into greater intimacy with Him. Praying prayers from the place of intimacy will create answers for others to live inside of.

Intercession flowing out of intimacy with God was desperately important to the way Jesus lived and the culture that He cultivated for His friends. As we move on to the last section of *Culture of the Few*, we will look at how Jesus modeled a life of *Intimacy* with the Father as He walked the earth, and how His relationship with the Father impacted the way He did relationships with people.

SECTION V
intimacy

15

knowing Father

Way back in chapter one, I said that this book is about how cultural transformation takes place. Since then, we have examined the life of Jesus—the ultimate agent of change—and what it was that allowed Him to impact the world around Him while primarily focusing most of His time on a handful of seemingly ordinary men. In each section of this book, we have looked at a different key to the *Culture of the Few* and studied how it impacted the way that Jesus lived, led and loved.

We started with *Identity* and said that because Jesus knew who He was, He was free to live His life without bowing to the expectations of what others thought Messiah should be. He was a Son satisfied to belong to the Father, doing only what He saw the Father do.

We moved on to examine the spirit of *Invitation* resting on the life of Jesus. Because He knew who He was, He was free to welcome others to belong with Him, follow Him, and ultimately give up their lives for Him.

In the midst of the pressures of the crowds that wanted to see Him, touch Him, and climb into the boat, we studied how Jesus grew His relationships with His disciples by living a life of *Intentionality*. This allowed Him to focus on and invest Himself into His few, trusting the seed of His life to be multiplied within them. This intentional investment of Himself was His plan for discipling the nations.

Lastly, we looked behind the scenes, away from the crowds and the events of Jesus' life to better understand His commitment to *Intercession*. Jesus regularly took time to both *see the Father and see with the Father*, which then enabled Him to pray the prayers that were on the Father's heart.

We spent quite a bit of time discussing how this life of intercession was connected to the high value that Jesus had for walking in Intimacy with the Father. As we move into this final key to the *Culture of the Few*, is there anything left to talk about? After all, we have spent most of the book referring to the important but simple fact that Jesus only did what He saw the Father doing, and He only said what He heard the Father say.

Did this one truth about the way Jesus lived really impact every area of His life? Is it possible that I, the author of this little book, have simply gotten distracted by one aspect of Jesus' life and am overemphasizing it to prove a point? It is, but let me assure that this was not the book that I set out to write.

I intended to talk about this truth as one of a short list of important things for us to learn from the life of Jesus, but must admit that I have been astounded at how my efforts to draw away from the subject—to "move on to something else"—have been thwarted at every turn. I can't escape it. From beginning to end and everything in between, the life of Jesus was centered on knowing the Father.

Even from the age of twelve, when He sent Mary and Joseph on a wild Christ-chase during the Passover Festival, Jesus was about His Father's business. Looking at and taking interest in what the Father was doing was not a technique that Jesus used to perform more miracles, or pray better prayers. It was central to everything that He did because it was the whole reason He came to the planet.

Wait! I can almost see the objection forming in the back of your mind. Didn't Jesus come to save us?

Yes, He came as God's plan of salvation; but as we have discussed, that plan was about restoring us into right relationship with the Father. Jesus came to bring us to relationship with God by showing us what it means to walk in relationship with His Father.

Some would also say that Jesus came to destroy the works of the devil, which is also true. But when we think about what the works of the devil really are, they are about disrupting our relationship with God and interrupting the benefits of what it means to walk that out.

So no—I don't think the topic of intimacy is being overemphasized. It really is that important. It really is that central to everything else in the life of Jesus.

In this section, we will look at how intimacy with the Father directed the way that Jesus interacted with His few and why choosing a lifestyle of intimacy is an "unskippable" essential for every "would-be world-changer." We will also look at what it means for us to adjust our lives to make room to be close with God.

the music changes

It is fun watching my daughter when she watches a movie—fun and sometimes frustrating. She really gets into things. If she has seen a movie before, she has a hard time not talking about what is about to happen. If she has not seen the movie we are watching, her curious mind will produce a question every 14.7 seconds. No matter how many times we tell her to be quiet and wait to see what happens, her curiosity continues to work and come up with new questions.

Then there is the part of the movie, usually near the end, when the music changes to build climactic suspense. In these moments, it is not uncommon for Abigail to get up and leave the room. She knows that something big is getting ready to happen, but because she doesn't know how the script will end, she gets nervous that things won't end up right and the movie will be ruined.

Have you ever heard the suspenseful music begin to play in the story of your life? Do you recognize those moments when you know something significant is about to happen, yet you don't know exactly how things will work out? These moments can be scary if we don't know the One who is writing the script, or our place in His story.

As Jesus transitioned into the last few days of His life, you can almost hear the music changing. The last week included a meal with friends, Mary anointing his feet, the excitement that surrounded the triumphal entry and preparations for Passover. He had overturned tables at the temple, wept over Jerusalem, and cursed a fig tree.

While He did not have a copy of the script, He was in close relationship with the Author and Director of the story. He was aware of the prophecies that told how His life would end, and He knew that the end was near.

Now before the Feast of the Passover, when Jesus knew that His hour had come that He should depart from this world to the Father, having loved His own who were in the world, He loved them to the end.[61]

These verses set the stage for what we know as the Last Supper. But when Jesus had told the disciples to prepare for dinner, He didn't call it that. He simply told them to make the usual preparations for the Passover meal. Scripture doesn't tell us exactly what Jesus knew about His final days, it just says that He *knew His hour had come.*

It was an hour that was bittersweet for Jesus. Just a little while later He would pray until sweat and blood ran from Him, asking the Father if there was any other way to accomplish that thing that He had come to earth for. His prayer was full of authentic fervency, yet He concluded with a humble surrender to the will of the Father.

The bitterness of the death that He would face was not because He was in love with His own life—He had already laid that down. The bitterness was because of the separation that He would experience from the One with whom He was inseparable as the weight of the sin of the world was placed on His sinless shoulders.

But there was also a sweetness in this hour, for in its coming it signified the transition of this world out of separation from the Father and back into His perfect presence. In one of the most magnificent parts of the story of God's love for mankind, the only begotten Son had left His home with Father to come and make His home with us. Now it was to time to depart the earth that He had created to return back to the throne room, and behind Him Jesus left a bridge that granted access to all who would follow Him.

---

61   John 13:1-3

Within all that glory, I believe there was a healthy tension in the heart of Jesus that night. On one hand there was a pull on His heart to finish what He had come to earth to do—to reconcile man to God, and then go home to be reunited perfectly with the Father. On the other hand, He had found a perfect love for the ones He had invited to come follow Him on the shoreline of the Sea of Galilee three years earlier.

John, who refers to himself as the disciple whom Jesus loved, gives us a snapshot into the upper room that night. I imagine dim lighting and hushed music as Jesus spends one last meal together with His few.

And supper being ended, the devil having already put it into the heart of Judas Iscariot, Simon's son, to betray Him, Jesus, knowing that the Father had given all things into His hands, and that He had come from God and was going to God, rose from supper and laid aside His garments, took a towel and girded Himself. After that, He poured water into a basin and began to wash the disciples' feet, and to wipe them with the towel with which He was girded.[62]

What would it be like to know that the heart of one of these men He had journeyed thousands of miles with would soon betray Him? He had invested everything in these twelve. What would it take for Him to rise up from His supper and humble Himself, to take on the form of a simple servant and wash the feet of His disciples, including the one who would hand Him over?

In the midst of John's description of these events, there is a phrase that points to what empowered Jesus to act with such a courageous love.

Jesus, knowing that the Father had given all things into His hands…

---

knowing the Father

Jesus—the One for whom the crowds had cried "Hosanna!" only a few days prior—was able to disrobe and wash the feet of His betrayer because of the confidence that came from knowing the Father. Because the Father had given all things into His hands, Jesus was able to give Himself freely to those who didn't deserve it, regardless of the consequences. This is how we see Intimacy impacting the way Jesus lived out the culture of the few. It was the closeness that He experienced with the One who ordered His steps that allowed Him to approach the final moments of His life with courage, grace, and humility.

Peter. Andrew. James. John. Phillip. Bartholomew. Thomas. Matthew. James the Less. Thaddeus. Simon. Judas Iscariot.

To Jesus, these were more than the names of the twelve apostles. These were His friends. These were the men that He had chosen to share His life with. For three years He had given Himself, day in and day out, to these unschooled, ordinary men. These unlikely world-changers were the ones that He had handpicked to pass the baton to. These were the ones that He loved to the end.

So when He had washed their feet, taken His garments, and sat down again, He said to them, "Do you know what I have done to you? You call Me Teacher and Lord, and you say well, for so I am. If I then, your Lord and Teacher, have washed your feet, you also ought to wash one another's feet."[63]

Jesus had played tag with His disciples before. They had heard Jesus, the Light of the World, tell them, "You are the light of the world." There had been times that He sent them out in pairs to go and practice the life He had modeled for them, but something seemed different now.

---

63   John 13:12-14

tag, you're it

"Do you know what I have done to you?" He had asked them after He finished loving and serving them. In this last meal that He would spend before His suffering, Jesus set a standard of what following Him should look like.

So what exactly *did* Jesus do to His disciples? We have already read that it was knowing the Father that enabled Him to rise from the table and serve the twelve, but in doing that He was essentially saying, "Do you see Me as your Master and Lord? Then you should do to each other what I have done for you." Jesus' actions flowed out of a new standard for the level of intimacy His disciples would need to have with the Father in order to carry out His works after He was gone, since Jesus was only able to operate with such selfless love because He knew the Father and what the Father was doing.

It is easy for me to believe that Jesus walked in perfect communion with the Father, and that the perfectness of that relationship is what allowed Him to move in such power and authority, but this thought process makes following Jesus seem impossible as my own relationship in communion with the Father so grossly fails in comparison. Yet when Jesus asks, "Do you know what I've done to you?" He is explicitly saying that the standard of life that He was leaving as an example for His disciples was one that flowed from and would require real intimacy with the Father. So the real question is, would He really invite them into something they could never hope to experience?

I am not saying that you or I or we will ever attain to that perfect level of intimacy and communion that Jesus, the One who knew no sin, experienced as he walked on this earth, but we cannot use this fact as an excuse. Why? Because in becoming our sin, Jesus said that He gave us access to the very throne room of God so that we might experience and grow in communion with His Father. The fact that we are seated together in heavenly realms in Christ must become less of a lofty theology that seems more fairytale than reality and more of a daily experience of our Christian lives. To restore us to an active, living, intimate relationship with His Father is a HUGE part of the reason Jesus died.

So the life of intimacy that Jesus lived out in front of His disciples became an important part of what He was expecting them to live out after He was gone. He paid the price to give them access to the Father by laying down His own life. He called them to live an impossible lifestyle that would require that they knew how to recognize what the Father was doing. And the same is true of us.

Of all the key components that we've looked at so far, intimacy is the one that we can most easily dismiss. But in reality, intimacy is most essential because it was the most integral part of Jesus' ministry. Out of his identity as a son, Jesus lived the life of closeness with the Father.

16

closing the circuit

Culture of the Few begins with knowing who you are *(Identity)* and ends with knowing why you are alive *(Intimacy)*. It is important that we learn how to connect our identities as sons and daughters of God into a lifestyle of seeking His face. I'm sure that this seems like a no-brainer to many of you, but surprisingly, a grasp of identity does not always lead to a cultivation of an intimate relationship with God.

I remember having a conversation with a son of a well-known leader in the church. We were sitting at dinner discussing spiritual inheritance, and why it often seems like there is a difficulty in seeing spiritual momentum stewarded from one generation to the next. As someone who has studied revival and modern church history, I was aware that many of the great moves of God throughout the last several hundred years have come to an end when one of two things happened: Either the older generation would reject and attack what God was doing in the younger generation; or the sons and daughters raised up in a move of God would become lazy and complacent, and the revival would seem to fizzle out.

We talked about how it seemed that princes had a choice in how they stewarded their sonship. If they embraced complacency and entitlement, it was likely that their influence would be diminished, and that their impact would be minimal. But if a son of the king could appreciate his sonship and live with a desire to see his father's kingdom expand, that "increase" and "honor" would be the words used most often in describing his life.

Being a son or a daughter of the Most High God is an honor, and one that should never be taken lightly. It is not because of our own merit that we have been born of the Spirit and adopted into His family; it is by His grace, and with a great price, that we have been rescued from the kingdom of darkness and despair and brought into the rule and reign of the Kingdom of God. But whenever I teach on the topic of identity, I always know there is a risk that it will become a reason for people to embrace entitlement due to our immaturity.

Identity means that we belong in the Father's house, that we have access to all that is His.

He who did not spare His own Son, but delivered Him up for us all, how shall He not with Him also freely give us all things?[64]

Although we have access to the Father, that does not mean we have intimacy. No, intimacy is something that grows intentionally. While there is nothing that we can do to earn more of God's love, purposely making room to see the Father and spending time in His presence opens us up to receive more of the boundless love that He has for us. He wants to pour more grace into our lives than we can fathom, but there is an undeniable connection in Scripture between receiving grace and seeking the face of God.

---

64   Romans 8:32

grace and face

Throughout the years, a standard definition for grace has become *unmerited favor*. This is not a bad definition, but it is an incomplete one. It is true that there is nothing that I can do to merit or earn God's grace. It is completely a gift from His heart. But the connection between "grace and face" in Scripture is also important to note. If you look at the word grace or favor in the Old Testament, you will find that an overwhelming number of the times that they are mentioned are connected with either the face or the eyes of the Lord.

But Noah found favor in the eyes of the LORD.[65]

May the Lord bless you and keep you and cause His face to shine upon you.[66]

In the light of the king's face there is life, and his favor is like a cloud of latter rain.[67]

When You said, "Seek My face," My heart said to You, "Your face, Lord, I will seek."[68]

While there is nothing that I can do to earn more of God's grace, I can position myself to better receive as I spend time seeking His face. Could this be why God instructs us to seek Him, because He wants us to receive all that our access opens up to us? While it is essential to understand our identity as sons and daughters of God, it is equally important to continually cultivate intimacy in our relationship with Him.

---

65   Genesis 6:8
66   Numbers 24-26
67   Proverbs 16:15
68   Psalms 27:8

It is futile to try to cultivate intimacy without understanding identity, because we only have access to God through His Son. The Son has made a way for us to come to the Father. I will not spend time, then, explaining the folly of trying to perform our way into a close relationship with God. I will simply say that understanding the Father's perfect love for us is the invitation that allows us to develop a lifestyle of closeness with Him. When we understand this, cultivating a lifestyle of intimacy with the Father closes the circuit that becoming a son opens up. Intimacy with the Father becomes the chief operation of my identity as a child of God.

living from the overflow

What does this have to do with cultural transformation and changing the world? Everything. Accepting the invitation to walk in intimacy with the Father empowers us to live out the lifestyle of only doing what we see the Father doing that Jesus modeled for us in the last section on *Intercession*. It is the internal transformation that comes from this invisible lifestyle that actually fuels the cultural transformation around us. And because we always have access to the Father through intimacy and intercession, we always have access to fuel.

Unfortunately, throughout history we've seen burnout claim the spiritual and physical lives of far too many world-changers. Some have said that these "brightest lights" were destined to burn out soon, but I wholeheartedly disagree. I do not believe that it is in the heart of a good Father to use up His children.

Can you imagine a father who ran a family business and worked his children twenty hours a day, depriving them of food and sleep and other essentials for living a healthy life? No matter how successful his children were or how profitable his business was, this type of parenting would be wrong. It would be a misuse of his authority and influence. It would be child abuse.

We would never take this type of behavior from a local business-man, yet somehow we have believed that living a perpetually unhealthy lifestyle is a part of the cost of being a radical world-changer for God. Whether it is the young and ambitious, or the old and tired, I have sat with far too many anointed men and women of God who have misunderstood the Father's good plans for their lives.

When we live in a spiritually dry land, it is easy to assume that any drop of water must be shared with anyone who will receive it. But I believe the testimony of David, the man after God's own heart, shows us a more perfect picture of the way that the Father wants us to live. In the 23rd Psalm, David, the shepherd-boy, gives us a beautiful picture of what his experience with God has been like. From reflecting on the security that accompanies knowing that he belongs, to recounting the many ways in which the Good Shepherd lovingly cares for him, David describes what it looks like to be well-taken care of and lacking nothing.

As a man who had known plenty of adversity in his life and had faced many adversaries on the battlefield, David said that the Good Shepherd prepared a banquet table for him in the presence of his enemies. He described being anointed with oil and how his cup overflowed in abundance. I believe that this description gives an accurate representation of the Father's heart for us all. In the midst of our battlefields, He has prepared a table for us. He pours out His Spirit upon us and has a plan for our hearts to live in a constant state of more-than-enough.

One of the most important things that every would-be world-changer needs to know is that God's plan is not for you to be poured out and empty. It is good to have a heart to share every good thing that God wants to give to us, but in a dry and weary land the best way to bring a flood is to learn how to remain in the place where He fills our cup to overflow.

This has been one of the most difficult challenges of my life. Whether I've experienced burnout or have backslidden, I recognize that a very natural reaction for me, when I encounter God again, is to run out and try to find someone to pour out on. Maybe there's a shred of generosity in my thirsty heart, but I truly believe that this desire to go share with others is a symptom of my need to have something to give.

I remember after seven years of pastoring that little church in North Carolina, when it came time for my wife and I to transition Pennsylvania, I found myself tired and thirsty. I was fortunate enough to find some friends who pointed me to the secret place, urging me to spend time with the Father. I must admit that in the business of pastoring, there had not been a lot of room for spending time with God that wasn't connected to preparing for some type of ministry. Whether a sermon prep, praying for our church members, or trying to get vision for our church's future, an overwhelming majority of the time that I spent with God could be characterized as trying to get something from Him so I had something to share with other people.

I remember going to the office I had set up in my house to pray one morning. I had already resigned from the church in North Carolina, but we still had a few weeks to go before moving to Pennsylvania. I had woken up early to spend time with God, but had determined that I didn't want that time to be focused on getting vision for what life and ministry would look like in Pennsylvania. It was a quiet time—not so much because I had embraced resting in His presence, but because it felt awkward and uncomfortable to have time with God that wasn't focused on getting something from Him.

While I lay on the floor in the silence, a picture popped into my mind. It was a cup. It looked normal enough at first, but then I saw hands reach down and begin to grab at its rim. The Hands pulled the rim outward, transforming the cup into what looked like an upside down bell whose top was now infinitely wider than the bottom. I remember asking the Lord, "What is this all about?"

I want to increase your capacity to receive.

Immediately I understood the meaning of the picture. I guess the fact that I determined to spend time with God without trying to get something that I could share with others indicates that I was already walking under a conviction from the Holy Spirit about developing greater intimacy with God. I knew from the picture of the cup that He was inviting me to know Him more, and receive more love from Him because it brought Him pleasure for me to be with Him and to spend time with Him.

I also recognized, through the image of the cup, that if God was making it a priority to increase my capacity to receive, then I needed to as well. This thought brought a wave of refreshing over my body. During the seven years I had spent pastoring, I had developed a very unhealthy schedule.

I worked full days, and had something to do almost every night. The first year that I was married, the only time that I had off came because the other pastor that I worked with insisted that I needed one day a week at home. It wasn't that I didn't want to spend time with my new wife, or make building our family a priority; it was the inner need to get everything done that presented itself as urgent or important that kept me away.

I was taking night classes at seminary. I was leading the church's youth group and young adult ministry. I led worship and preached Sundays on a regular basis. And on top of all this, for most of my time at that church I had a second job. It was not as if I felt obligated by others to have to keep such a schedule; it was part of what I thought I said yes to when I said yes to ministry. God was doing good things, and we were blessed to see many people come to Jesus during those years.

While I did not have a grasp on the fabric of what discipleship really was yet, it was during this season of seeing hundreds of people say yes to Jesus that I started to catch the concept of intentionally investing into their lives. Unfortunately, I tried to add a lot of one-on-one discipleship meetings into my schedule without taking anything out. I was on the verge of burnout.

My busy schedule became a badge, worn to show the sacrifice of the cost of being a world-changer. Even though I was worn out by my attempts to keep up with all that God was doing, I was determined as we entered into this transition from North Carolina to Pennsylvania to continue to go hard after God.

That early morning encounter with the Father, where I began to see my need to receive from Him, became a life-changing moment for me. It was during that transition that I recognized the ways I had neglected my wife, hoping that there would be some scraps left over for her after I had spent time pouring into everyone else. Again, let me be very clear: My neglect for my wife was not out of a heart to devalue her, but because I thought it was my responsibility to get something from God and go pour it out on whoever would receive it.

As I look at the heart of God as revealed by David in that psalm, I recognize that God is not looking for me to leave the place of His outpouring so that I can go take a little water to someone in need. It is the heart of God that I learn to live from the overflow, allowing Him to fill up my life to a place were His abundance spills over onto the lives of others around me.

There are still times when I get tired, but now I have permission to rest. I no longer have an obligation to pour out my life at the expense of my own heart. He makes me lie down in green pastures, He leads me beside still waters. He restores my soul.[69]

This is really good news—that the God of heaven cares about your soul in a way that deeply impacts the way He leads your life. He wants you to lie down and have rest in a place where you can eat from His fresh provision. He wants you to drink deep and always know that He has more where that came from. Restoration is His priority for your life.

As you embrace a life of following Jesus, you will be faced with the opportunity to become overwhelmed by the needs of the world. You will see needs everywhere around you. You will see poverty in the nations and brokenness in your neighborhood. Even in the lives of your few, you will be faced with the reality of your own limitations.

In the midst of this reality, remember the importance of intimacy. Not so that you will have something to give to everyone else, but so you can continually come back to that place of knowing that the Father has more than enough for you. Resist the urge to get something good from God and then run out and share it with anyone who will listen. Instead, learn to find a place in your life where you can position your heart to receive from Him. Allow Him to pour into your life, seeing the value that He places on your heart, and then trust Him to refresh others out of that overflow.

---

69   Psalms 23:2

17

it's all about Jesus

Shortly after moving to Western Pennsylvania in 2002, I was intro-duced to Jim and Jan Erb. They had been pioneers in the Jesus move-ment back in the 70's and had provided ministry oversight to many lead-ers around our region. While I was more than happy to meet them, I had no way of knowing that Jim and Jan would become mentors and spiritual parents for my wife and me.

I have learned many things from this wonderful couple, but it was a lesson that I learned back in those early years of our relationship that has made the biggest impact in my life. Jim had already been in min-istry for nearly fifty years when I met him, and his resume' included pastoring small rural churches, being a missionary to the Philippines, pioneering new church plants, and overseeing an international network of ministries and missionaries through an organization he had founded to support other leaders. It seemed like everywhere I went throughout Western Pennsylvania or Eastern Ohio, I met someone who knew Jim Erb.

Shortly before I had met him, he had gone through what he describes as "the dark night of the soul." He had been traveling a lot, speaking and teaching throughout the US and internationally. Because of the extensive travels, he had stepped away as the senior pastor from the church that he had led for two decades. This transition was difficult for Jim as he struggled to understand exactly what his purpose would be.

As Jim sat at his house, he wrestled with what was next for him in terms of his life and ministry. He and Jan had been on the go for decades, raising their children and giving their lives to following Jesus in ministering to others. Now that that season was ending, Jim did not have a clear sense of what was next. In the midst of this time he also developed some health issues that added to his wonderings.

In the midst of this uncertainty, God met Jim in his favorite chair as he would cry out and wait on the Lord. It was not a short wait, but over time Jim began to sense that his greatest ministry was before him. But for a man who had led Jesus festivals that drew tens of thousands of young hippies to a rural Pennsylvanian farm, what greater ministry could there be?

As Jim sat and waited, he began to gain understanding about just how precious the sitting and waiting was. Quite different from his life on the go, now he would sit alone with the Lord for hours at a time. He would often awaken in the middle of the night to go worship and spend time with God. As he would sit in his chair or pace back and forth in his living room, Psalm 27:4 became the cry of his heart.

One thing I have desired of the Lord, that will I seek: That I may dwell in the house of the Lord all the days of my life, to behold the beauty of the Lord, and to inquire in His temple.

As Jim began to build his life around living for this One Thing, he became newly aware that his greatest ministry on this earth would be unto the Lord Himself. It is not that Jim stopped ministering to people, but he did begin to prioritize spending time with the Father above all else. He likes to say that during this time, he resigned his position as "governor of the universe" and gave control back to God. As he did this, Jim found that he was consistently being drawn into greater depths of intimacy with Jesus and new levels of co-operation with the Holy Spirit. In this way, as Jim's focus shifted to ministering more to the Lord, he became more effective in ministry to people.

This is when I met Jim. I was in my late twenties and had just started "my own ministry." I was full of vision and ambition to change the world. While Jim encouraged my passion, as our relationship grew, he consistently, lovingly sowed into me that lesson I mentioned at the beginning of the chapter that has so impacted my life:

"It's all about Jesus now," he would say. "It's not about your ministry or what you can accomplish for Him."

Of course, this sounded like one of those things that an older person is supposed to say when speaking to someone who is young and full of ambition. The first few times that he said it, I think I subconsciously dismissed the instruction. But the more that I got to know him, the more I heard the conviction in his voice. Jim went through all of his stories and shared with me the good things that he had seen God do throughout his life. But then he went on to say that the older he got, the more he realized that more than the accomplishments, more than all of the messages or miracles, that this life was all about Jesus.

I found this quite offensive to my "world-changer" mindset. Of course it's all about Jesus, but it must also be about how I can make a difference. As Jim repeated this truth to me over and over again, my heart began to understand that even more than accomplishing my calling, reaching my potential, or fulfilling my destiny, the ultimate purpose of the Father in my life is actually to make me more like Jesus.

the power of beholding

As we have already said, the key to following Jesus into a life of intimacy is found in seeking the face of the Father. When we make living for *One Thing* the highest aim of our lives, we are making a priority of living life from His presence.

It seems a bit embarrassing to admit, but somehow it is easy for us to miss this priority in our attempts to do something significant for God. In my own life, I spent years trying to learn how to "do more and sin less" so that I could make a bigger impact in my ministry. Yes, it is both embarrassing and revealing to know that the motive of my heart can easily be influenced to try to create my own place in His story instead of being fully satisfied in simply knowing Him.

That is why the cry to live a *one thing* lifestyle is so powerful. In this model, I am actually coming to a place where I reserve my highest priority for intentionally seeking the face of the Father. It is offensive to my natural mind that this has more power to make me like Jesus than all of my own efforts could ever accomplish.

But we all, with unveiled face, beholding as in a mirror the glory of the Lord, are being transformed into the same image from glory to glory, just as by the Spirit of the Lord.[70]

When Paul spoke these words to the church of Corinth, I believe he gave us one of the most powerful insights in the entire New Testament.

---

70   2 Corinthians 3:18

We are used to David making these kinds of statements in the Psalms, but when Paul affirms that living for one thing is what produces real transformation in our own lives under the new covenant, he points us to the power of beholding the face of God.

Yes, this verse sounds mystical and even super-spiritual to an extent. After all, doesn't the Scripture also teach us that no one has seen the face of God and lived? But Paul was talking about something more than the physical encounter with a spirit being; he was showing us the fruit of having the eyes of our understanding opened and then choosing to spend time beholding Jesus, gazing into the glory of God.

I have a friend named John who has been a big influence in my life. He is a few years older than me and has been a big brother that I look up to in many ways. One of the greatest areas of his influence in my life has been that of consistently making time to spend with God. He often says that this beholding—or seeking the Father's face—is rarely crystal-clear. It is often dim and even uninspiring. But it is in developing a lifestyle of on-going glances and gazes into the face of our loving Father that we become more like Jesus. And that, after all, is what God is really up to in our lives.

More than my vision to reach the nations or my desire to raise up young leaders and send them out to take the gospel to every sphere of society for the glory of God, I believe that what God is interested in most is making me more like Jesus. As I recognize the priority in the life of Jesus to spend time beholding the Father, it becomes clear to me that following Jesus in the area of intimacy is not disconnected from what God wants to do in my life—it is the core of it.

Let us conclude this section on *Intimacy* with one simple thought: The most important purpose in my life is beholding the face of the Father, being transformed by His love into the image of His perfect Son.

conclusion

18

dream big, live small

Somewhere, in a box of old photos, there is a slightly wrinkled picture of me from college. I come across it every now and then while searching for Christmas decorations or old journals, and every time I do I can't help but chuckle. It is probably the most tangible piece of physical evidence from my own "would-be world-changer" days. It depicts me sitting next to one of the aging leaders of the movement of churches that I grew up in, a very serious look on my face. Both of us wore matching navy blue suits, white shirts and red ties. I am not sure what we could have been discussing that would have warranted such an intense-looking photo, but every time I see that image, it reminds me of how determined I was to do something big for God.

Back in the first chapter, I said that the idea of being a "world-changer" should be as natural as the sun rising in the East for a follower of Jesus. As we enter into the conclusion of this book, let's revisit that good, godly desire to make a big difference in the world. After looking at the life of Jesus and the process that He went through, I hope that the desire to follow and impact the world with Him has only grown!

Sometimes, the cost of the process can become an obstacle to seeing our dreams fulfilled, but don't let the threat of a high price prevent you from your desire to change the world. Let it instead speak to the value of what you are giving your life for.

Several years ago, I had the opportunity to hear a missionary speak about all of the things that she and her husband had seen God do as they co-labored with Him in one of the poorest nations in the world. They had set out to see the gospel work in the midst of some of the hardest circumstances on the earth. Of course, God showed up in and around the lives of this family in powerful ways, miraculously providing for the many orphans that they took in. And because of their faithfulness in taking care of the fatherless, their ministry became a distribution point for humanitarian relief efforts after huge storms had flooded their region. While the hungry stood in line waiting for food, the gospel was shared and thousands of people came to Jesus. They began to gather and train these new disciples and send them back to plant churches and take care of the fatherless in their villages.

The stories of blind eyes seeing, deaf ears being opened up, and even people being raised from the dead have spread around the world. On the night that I heard this missionary share her story, she said something relevant to our conversation that deeply impacted me.

People are always asking how they can see God move in their lives the way we see Him move. They say that they want what we have, but they don't know the cost.

If we are going to follow Jesus, the ultimate agent of change, it will always come with the cost of laying down our lives. For some, the cost seems more drastic than others, but all of us must answer the call to find our lives by losing them. It is in losing our own lives that we become free to really follow Jesus, the One who has given His life for ours.

Now remember, truly following Jesus is not the same as culturally following a religious system built in His honor. The heart of this book has been about taking a closer look at the life of Jesus and asking ourselves how we can actually follow Him by readjusting our values to be able to live like He lived. As we examined *Identity, Invitation, Intentionality, Intercession* and *Intimacy,* we take them as daily practices in, or the very essence of, the lifestyle of the One that we follow—not as a checklist of things to accomplish.

Our ability to be fruitful in this life flows from staying connected to the Vine. Yes, it is the seed of the life of Jesus in our own lives that has the power to produce the kind of change in us that we long to see happen around us—and that is ultimately the real key to sustainable cultural transformation.

As we prepare to land the plane on *Culture of the Few,* I want to leave you with a few practical thoughts that have been helpful in my journey of learning how to follow after Jesus.

go ahead and dream

When I was in college, the pastor of the church that I went to had a maxim that he quoted regularly. *Dream big dreams, pray big prayers and get ready to do big things with God.* I recognize that hearing that phrase repeated over and over again had a deep impact in my heart.

Even though I already wanted to change the world, my heart was encouraged by the call to dream big dreams. It was like the fence posts of my heart were being picked up and moved outward, as if the realm of what was possible was expanding beyond what I had previously thought.

Sometimes, when I call young, ambitious leaders to embrace life in the carpenter's shop, or to be patient in the process, it can almost feel like I am pouring cold water onto their dreams to change the world. I never want to be a dream killer, and so I pray that whatever water I do pour would not extinguish the fire, but rather nurture the soil of their hearts.

It is imperative that we recognize the importance of the things that we carry in our hearts for God, the things we dream about doing with and for Him. David had it in his heart to build a temple for God. It wasn't a command to obey or a prophecy to fulfill; it was a desire that he carried with him. And even though God would ultimately choose David's son Solomon to build that temple, David gave himself to preparing and making sure that every provision needed to finish it was in place.

At the dedication of the temple, Solomon remembered what had been in his father's heart and made it a point to mention it as a part of his prayer for God to come and fill the house. Of course, God did come and fill that temple with His presence, fulfilling the dream of David's heart.

Give yourself to dreaming big dreams with God—especially in the place of prayer—but then give yourself to the process of letting the seed of those dreams take root and grow to a place of maturity so it can bear fruit.

walking it out

I believe that as we follow Jesus, it is natural for these "dreams"[71] to form in our hearts. In Psalms 20:4 David writes:

May He grant you according to your heart's desire, and fulfill all your purpose.

---

71   When I speak of dreams, I am speaking about the desires that are formed in our hearts through prayer and communion with God. Often times, in our own immaturity, it is possible to begin to follow the dreams of our heart at the expense of following Jesus. It is sad when we see people live without any sense of dreams in their lives, but it is equally sad when we see people turn their dreams into idols.

There is something about what God has placed inside your heart that is connected to His purpose for your life, but we need to remember that recognizing the dream is just the beginning of the process.

Dreaming is a lot like conceiving in the sense that it is the starting point in bringing something life-giving to the earth. But what comes after conception is a lot of growth, development, and hard work. Once we can clearly recognize the desire that God is forming in us, we must learn how to carry it with us in patience and persistence until that dream becomes a reality.

I learned this during one of the most important paradigm shifts of my life. I was just starting to learn the value of the concepts of the Culture of the Few as I studied the life of Jesus, but I had never actually seen anyone do ministry that way. I felt so foolish as I dreamed of making an impact in the world by loving and discipling a few people at a time, who would in turn give themselves to making a few disciples. I kept going back and forth in my heart between the conviction of how I saw Jesus live and make disciples, and the perception of what it meant to be successful in modern ministry.

All that changed one morning at Jim Erb's house. He had invited Mark Geppert to come and share with us that day. Mark carried a strong burden for the people of Asia to know Jesus. He pioneered the South East Asia Prayer Center (SEAPC) in 1991 with a vision for saturating the region with prayer.

With a conviction that the dream in his heart to see Southeast Asia know Jesus was also the dream of God's heart, Mark literally began to walk out those dreams. He made a practice of spending weeks at a time "prayer walking" throughout the region during trips overseas. Mark traveled across Southeast Asia, walking and praying as the Holy Spirit directed, focusing prayer on specific places of influence.[72]

Tears flowed down my cheeks as I sat in the meeting listening to the stories of how God was moving in China, Laos, and Cambodia. It was clear that God was joining Mark in his prayer walks around Asia—or was it that Mark was joining God? My heart was encouraged to hear how Mark had met with leaders of the underground church in China and learned the strategy of discipling a handful of men at a time.

The Chinese did this in order to be able to multiply the gospel and equip leaders without drawing attention to themselves through large assemblies. What had started as a practical way of making disciples without interference from the communist government had led to a growing church, with new disciples multiplying like seeds in the wind.

Mark had taken what he learned in China and was teaching what he called the "Core Four" model of disciple making to leaders throughout the whole of Southeast Asia. The church in Cambodia was multiplying each year and the gospel was spreading like wildfire in Indonesia, the largest Muslim nation in the world.

My head was spinning as I heard Mark's stories of the gospel spreading in such places as disciples were free to intentionally invest their lives into a handful of new disciples. The stories of the faithfulness of the Asian church inspired me, as many of these new believers were paying a great price to follow Jesus. Some faced persecution from the government, while others were immediately disowned by their families. Yet the good news was spreading every day, through the lives of ordinary men and women who were walking out their new faith.

---

72   For more on Mark's prayer strategy, read his book: Geppert M. (2001). *Attack Lambs*. Genesis Publishing.

One story stood out to me that day as a great example of how to "Dream Big and Live Small." Mark was prayer walking in the Tibetan province of China. As he was focusing on the centers of influence in the area, he came across a giant stone Buddha. He sat down on a bench before the statue and began to silently pray for God to come and demonstrate His love and power to the people who walked under the darkness of Buddhism. As he prayed, Mark noticed a Buddhist monk on a bench next to him reading Buddhist prayers off of a Sanskrit prayer tile.

Mark asked God for an open door to share the gospel with this monk, and got the idea to hold out a pamphlet of literature about Jesus written in Tibetan—even though he didn't speak the language! Sure enough, the monk noticed Mark's "prayer tile," and when he saw that the monk was curious Mark gave it to him to read. Moments later, the monk began to weep and Mark suspected that he had just believed the good news and given his life to Jesus. Mark joined the monk in tears and they hugged, sharing several moments on the bench in awe of God's goodness.

A little while later, Mark was approached by a Chinese authority figure who had witnessed the display of kindness and affection on the bench and had been moved. He turned out to be the Public Health Director for all of Tibet, representing the communist Chinese government in that region. The director asked Mark and his organization if they would be interested in leading a public health project for Tibet, and Mark emphatically said, "Yes!" The director then told Mark about a group of children that suffered from a specific heart valve defect related to congenital heart disease.

What happened next is almost unbelievable. After a series of meetings and much more prayer, Mark signed a contract with the government that enabled SEAPC to coordinate researchers and medical professionals to examine and serve over 17,000 children in all of Tibet's seven prefectures. Mark got the approval of the government that every one of those families would be able to have a "support group" that SEAPC would help facilitate. Many of those support groups became small simple churches. The gospel spread through a Christian Missions Organization ministering in Communist China with the consent and blessing of the government!

After that initial project was done, Mark asked if there was anything else that he could do to serve the people in the province, and open doors came in the area of education and literacy. Years later, SEAPC still serves the people of China by helping to establish the protocol for treating autism in that country.

Mark had no idea all that would happen in the Tibetan province of China when he left his home in Oakmont, Pennsylvania to go prayer walk for a few weeks. He was just being faithful to follow Jesus and walk out the desires on his heart, believing that as he did, God would meet him and do what only God could do.

After meeting Mark, my heart had the fuel that it needed to make the culture of the few a reality in my own life. The stories of what God is doing through SEAPC continue to give me courage and hope that Jesus is still multiplying the seed of His life into small handfuls of ordinary men and women that are turning the world upside down for Him. Over the years, SEAPC has grown from its humble beginnings in Oakmont to having a presence in over 70 nations throughout Asia and around the world. They are seeing the gospel spread through prayer, church planting, and leadership development as they continue to engage these nations through platforms like health, education, and providing for the fatherless.[73]

---

73   seapc.org

i know who goes before me

There is one last truth I want to leave with you. As we recognize what we carry in our hearts and learn how to walk those things out in the midst of everyday life, it is important to remember that the real hope for changing the world does not rest on our shoulders. This can be hard for our hearts to remember. In the midst of our desires to make an impact, sometime it can become easy to take on pressure and responsibility that really belong to Jesus.

One of the main reasons that I wanted to write this book was because I saw young leaders who had hearts to change the world for Jesus, suffering from some common conditions. Many were burning out from trying to get into their destinies without walking through the process that God had designed to make them ready. Others were buckling under the weight of the visions that they were carrying. We are susceptible to both of these when we forget that it is not by our might or by our own power that God works, but by His Spirit.[74] It is not by fulfilling my prophetic words or by reaching my potential that anything truly world-changing will happen. Exercising my leadership strength and executing my best missions strategies will not bring the nations to Jesus. No, these things—and every thing else that will matter in eternity—happen only by the Spirit of God.

Yes, it is God's good pleasure to co-operate with me in seeing His Kingdom come to earth, but the weight of changing the world rests squarely upon the shoulders of Jesus.

For unto us a Child is born,

Unto us a Son is given;

And the government will be upon His shoulder.

And His name will be called

---

74   Zechariah 4:6

Wonderful, Counselor, Mighty God,

Everlasting Father, Prince of Peace.

Of the increase of His government and peace

There will be no end...[75]

This single revelation has provoked great hope and wonder in my heart over the years. Knowing that Jesus is both the Author and Finisher of this race has the power to propel us with courage into living an impossible life. I don't have to live fueled by the pressure to make something happen. I can be free to run with Jesus and trust that He is faithful and true.

He has invited me to walk with Him and to share in His burden for the nations. But as I join myself with Him, sharing His yoke, I recognize that He is bigger than I am. When I am properly joined with Him, the weight of the world rest upon His shoulders. This is the way He designed it.

When Isaiah said that *the government would rest upon His shoulder,* he was not talking about a political structure. The root of the Hebrew word for government used in Isaiah 9 means "the power to prevail." Isaiah goes on to say that the increase of this government is without end.

If it never stops increasing, that means it is always growing. When we allow the weight of what we are carrying to rest on His shoulders instead of carrying the pressure ourselves, we are really introducing the weight of the world to God's ever increasing power to prevail.

---

75   Isaiah 9:6-7a

When we insist on carrying the pressure ourselves, however, we miss out on God's provision of love for us and deprive others from seeing God's power revealed. He is the One that goes before us and does all of the heavy lifting. It's His pleasure to allow us to share in the victory as we cease from our labors and enter into His rest.

I have seen this truth at work as God has answered prayers that I had forgotten I had even prayed. Some of the greatest things I have ever seen God do have come in the midst of my most boneheaded moments, times when all I knew how to do was be present while He did all of the work.

It is humbling when God transforms our weakness into something great. To see the Father work through my own brokenness to bring people to Jesus, to watch Him open up the ears of the deaf in spite of my weariness has helped me remember that He is the One who possesses the power. And just like my earthly father so many years ago, it is His delight to bring me to work with Him.

So, it's all about Jesus—about His power and person and love. I don't need to be over-whelmed by the scope of what needs done, because I know that He goes before me and stands beside me. No giant is too tall to take on as long as I remember that the battle belongs to the Lord.

As I follow Jesus, allowing the dreams and desires of His heart to influence mine as I walk out the things that He has entrusted to me, I do so with the hope and confidence that He is with me, able to do exceedingly and abundantly beyond what I can ask, think, or imagine.

The ideas that are found in *Culture of the Few* do not lead us to reducing our dreams down to something manageable; they focus us toward the Life of Jesus, the One who empowers us to live the impossible. As we dream big and live small, we don't surrender ourselves to small-minded thinking. We don't settle for the status quo. No—we follow the ultimate agent of change, who came to this earth with the mammoth mission of redeeming a lost world to the Father. He then patiently waited in the carpenter's shop before the Father led Him to invest the last three years of His life on earth into a few ordinary men who would turn the world upside down.

19

one last world-changer story

In chapter one, I briefly mentioned a young man named Lee Myers. Lee was a passionate follower of Jesus who became a pioneer in a student church planting movement. I got to know Lee when he was a sophomore at Allegheny College. He had been connected to a campus ministry that focused a lot on creating fellowship for believers and doing monthly outreaches to students who didn't know about Jesus.

Lee was one of the leaders of this campus ministry, but he was struggling with the disconnect he saw between the way Jesus made disciples and the way he was leading the monthly outreaches. Somehow, Lee had heard some testimonies about how my small tribe was trying to make disciples and reached out to me to see if we could meet up.

When Lee called me for the first time, I had no way of knowing that he would become such an important part of our family and our journey with Jesus. All I knew was that this young man had a desire for his campus to know Jesus, and I wanted to do whatever I could to help. I agreed to meet with him for breakfast. We passed the morning sharing stories and getting to know one another. The afternoon rolled around as he began to share his heart for his classmates. Before I knew it, we had spent the whole day talking, dreaming and praying for Lee's campus.

My heart was so encouraged in meeting this young man. I agreed to come visit him and pray with him on his campus the following month. Again, I had no way of knowing what God was about to do—I was just glad to come alongside a young leader and help in whatever way I could.

When I showed up the next month to pray with Lee on his campus, I saw why Lee was so burdened. While there were several strong Christian fellowships on campus, most of the students did not know Jesus and were not interested in attending any sort of nice Christian meetings.

"We keep renting the gym, ordering pizza and playing volleyball, hoping that if people show up enough they will figure out that they are missing something," Lee said. "I just want them to see Jesus…"

As time passed, our connection with Lee grew. He decided to come do a summer internship with us between his sophomore and junior year. His passion was to study the life of Jesus and then follow Him the best he knew how. This passion led Lee way out of his comfort zone.

As he read the gospels, he became convicted about the way he saw Jesus minister to people who were sick, hurting, and in need. I remember Lee calling one day to tell me that he had just read all of the stories of Jesus and the book of Acts and was blown away by how God's power changed peoples' lives. He asked me to hold him accountable to pray for people whenever he saw something was wrong.

"I don't know if I have the gift of healing or anything, but I can at least ask God to come and show up for the person," he said. "So if I am in a room and I see something that Jesus would take care of, I am going to ask Him too."

Such *simple faith*, I thought to myself. "Sure, I will hold you accountable."

I hung up and wondered how long Lee's experiment would last.

"Guess what?" he exclaimed when I answered the phone the next day. "God healed someone on campus today!"

"Wow," I said. "That's great!"

I wasn't completely surprised. We had been training people to pray for the sick and hurting for several years by that point, and expected that God wanted to show His love and power to people.

But then came a phone call the next day, and then again a few days later. With each call, Lee's excitement grew as he told us testimonies of what God was doing on his campus. There were dozens of physical healings taking place as the good news about what Jesus was doing was beginning to spread. Athletes began showing up at Lee's dorm when they were injured.

But God was doing more than healing people's bodies. Atheists and Buddhists started becoming intrigued by what was happening. They started showing up at the small, simple church gatherings that Lee had started in his dorm room, too. All of a sudden, these students that Lee had been burdened for the year before began giving their lives to Jesus.

This move of God continued throughout the semester. Lee and a few of his friends began to chronicle all of the testimonies into what they called "The Acts at Allegheny." The following semester, the simple church that Lee had started multiplied several times. There were people meeting in several dorm rooms, reading the Word, praying and worshipping. Soon, a simple church started in one of the frat houses, and then one started to meet at a local restaurant.

The word began to spread to other campuses in our region. Lee would go meet with other student groups and encourage them with the testimonies of what God had been doing at Allegheny. Before long, an informal network of students from eight or nine campuses began to track together. They would get together once a month or so to share reports of what was happening on each campus and pray for each other.

I was amazed at what was happening, and so glad to be a part of it. I thought, *If this is what God is doing in this generation, I wouldn't be born anytime else.* It was during this season that we began to become aware of other pockets of similar things happening across the country. Lee and I were so excited to see what would happen next.

a bump in the road

One thing that I have yet to mention is that Lee was diagnosed with a form of bone cancer as a high school junior. Doctors had found a tumor in his left leg and after several rounds of treatment, had decided to replace his femur with a titanium rod. Lee continued to get checked on for the next several years. There were times when it seemed like cancer was in Lee's rearview mirror, that it was a part of his past. But then a scan would come back with a spot on his lung or some other cause for concern.

Lee had determined not to allow cancer to control his life, and it looked pretty normal for the first few years after we met. That all changed during the first semester of his senior year of college. Something was going on in his left leg again. He tried not to let it bother him at first, but he began to experience a lot of pain.

It was difficult for all of us to watch our friend, whom God had used to bring physical healing to so many people, now struggle with the pain of the growing tumor aggressively attacking his body. We fasted and prayed and did everything that we knew to do to see Lee experience healing.

The first half of 2007 was one of the most difficult times of my life. I felt helpless as my friend and spiritual son suffered. And while it seemed like we were on the verge of regional revival just months before, now we were fighting for our friend's life tooth and nail.

Lee had to drop out of his last semester at college when the pain became unbearable. After months of praying and waiting, he decided to schedule a surgery to remove his left leg. Even after the surgery was scheduled, we prayed and believed that God would touch Lee. When the day of the surgery came, we all prayed that God would remove the tumor in front of the surgeon's eyes.

When I received the call to let me know that the surgery had been "a success"—that they had removed Lee's leg and that the doctors thought they had gotten rid of the entire tumor—I wasn't quite sure how to react. How could this have happened? This is not the way that the story was supposed to go.

When I first went to the hospital to visit Lee, I was immediately impressed that he hadn't lost hope or his passion to follow Jesus. Don't get me wrong; there were many difficult days as he transitioned to a physical rehabilitation center to adjust to his new situation. There were times of intense frustration and doubt, but for the most part, Lee was determined to get back to living life.

Just two weeks after he was released from the hospital, Lee spoke at a friend's church. The title of his message was "The Spirit Stayed In." It was healing for many of us to hear Lee testify to the fact that even in losing his leg, God had been faithful to him.

Lee began to record his journey on his blog, writing about life, his battle with cancer, and following Jesus. He became even more determined to pray for the sick and share the good news about Jesus. By the fall, he was driving again and felt hopeful about the future.

During the next few months, Lee experienced many ups and downs, but he carried a belief deep in his heart that God had His hand on his life, that God was going to use him to change the world. Lee was definitely a world-changer, and this type of thinking only proved it.

While there were still some physical setbacks to deal with, Lee seemed to be hitting his stride again. He began to travel some and share his story. In the summer of 2008, he traveled to Lawrence, Kansas for the first Student Church Planting Experience—a two-week training that focused on equipping college students to live like missionaries on their campuses.

Lee was excited to learn from missional leaders from across the country and to share his church planting stories from his time at Allegheny. When it came time for the students to go out on assignments, Lee was right there with them, crutching his way up and down the streets of Lawrence. His experience at that first SCPx encouraged him, because he had met other young followers of Jesus who were just as determined as he was to change the world.

Lee did change the world, but it was not in the way that we all expected. Within just a few months of his time in Lawrence, the cancer came back with a vengeance. I was actually in Las Vegas at a meeting with many of those same world-changers that Lee had met at SCPx when I got word that he had taken a turn for the worse.

I flew home to visit Lee in the hospital. We talked together and prayed. He asked me to read him stories about Jesus from the gospel, and then he wanted to worship. By this time, Lee had lost a lot of weight and many systems in his body were starting to shut down. With a weak voice, Lee began to sing to Jesus.

Take my life,
You can have it all,
I am Yours...

As I sat there in the hospital room at the bedside of my friend, I began to sob. I had tried to hold it together as long as I could, but this was just too much. While I believed that God was still able to raise Lee up from this deathbed, I knew as I drove home that Sunday afternoon that my friend's days on this earth were few, outside of a miracle.

The next day, Lee's father called and asked if I could come to the hospital. The doctors had told the family that they did not think Lee would make it through the afternoon. As I entered the hospital, it seemed like the day that we had been praying against for so long had come at last.

When I walked into the room, I saw Lee surrounded by his parents and a few friends. His breathing was shallow and it seemed as if he could slip away from this life at any moment. We were there together for a few hours when we all sensed Lee breathing his last few breaths.

I closed my eyes, asking God to come and show His power. As I did, I had what I can only describe as a vision. I have not had many in my lifetime, but the details are just as vivid today as they were years ago. In my vision, I saw Lee rounding the final turn in what seemed like an Olympic race. He was running with two legs.

The stadium was full of spectators and the flashbulbs of cameras lit up the whole arena. As Lee rounded the bend, I noticed that he was carrying a baton in his hand. I looked up towards the finish line, and there, waiting with outstretched arms, was Jesus. I will never forget the look on His face as He waited for Lee to cross the finish line and complete his leg of the race.

As Lee got closer to Jesus, two things happened simultaneously. First, Lee let go of the baton. It remained there, suspended in air, and I saw two words written on it, one at either end. On one end was the word power and on the other was written the word simplicity.

At the same time, Lee crossed the finish line and ran right into the arms of Jesus. I couldn't see Lee's face, but I could see the face of Jesus clearly. He was so happy and so full of joy.

In my vision, I recognized what was happening in the hospital room. I was aware that Lee had slipped from this world into the arms of Jesus. I looked at Jesus, and I looked at the baton. I looked back at Jesus and asked, "What do I do? What do I do with this baton?"

Pick it up and run, He said. *Call others to run with it, too.*

running with the baton

I must admit that it feels pretty vulnerable to share Lee's journey with you. As you can imagine, that story is intensely personal and still feels fresh as I write it. For all of the vulnerability and emotion, you might be wondering why I chose to share it at all. What does Lee's journey have to do with the culture of the few?

Much like the story I shared with you in chapter one about Donna Bishop, the impact of Lee's life and death has been monumental in my life and in the lives of many others.

In the days following Lee's death, I received phone calls from friends and ministry leaders from across the country. They were calling to express their condolences and to let me know that they were praying for us. Many of them also encouraged me about the impact that Lee's life was already having.

Several of them said that Lee's life had drawn them to the words of Jesus in John 12:24.

Most assuredly, I say to you, unless a grain of wheat falls into the ground and dies, it remains alone; but if it dies, it produces much grain.

God has taken the seed of Lee's life and multiplied it beyond my wildest expectations. Lee's story encouraged college students around the nation to follow Jesus and make disciples on their campuses. These students have now all graduated, but many of them continue to live out what they learned on their campuses in the neighborhoods and workplaces where they do life now.

For some, that has meant moving into the inner city, while others have gone out to the nations. Many have moved back to the small towns that they came from. Wherever they are, there remains an invitation to pick up the baton and run the race.

As the students that heard Lee's story and were inspired to follow hard after Jesus have grown up and made disciples, it is unlikely that many of those new disciples have ever heard of Lee. And as those new disciples have grown into disciple makers, they most certainly have not passed on the details to a part of their own story that they don't even know. And yet the impact of the life of an ordinary follower of Jesus continues to expand.

That is the lesson from Lee's life: that we can trust the seed of Christ to work, whether things turn out the way that we think they should or not. The conviction that Lee lived with—that God's hand was on his life, and that God wanted to use him to change the world—was not wrong. Though very few people will ever know his name, it doesn't matter; there is an undeniable impact in the lives of those that knew him, and it continues to grow today in those they've gone on to disciple. Just like in the story of Donna from chapter one, an extraordinary impact was made through an ordinary young person who had been with Jesus.

And that, after all, is what this book is all about. The hope for cultural transformation does not come from us reaching our potential or making names for ourselves. It doesn't come from getting credit for something good or for coming up with a clever strategy. The hope for cultural transformation comes from the lives of courageous people who carry transformation inside of them, allowing their lives to spill over on others. These courageous people live their lives trusting that their investment into a handful will be multiplied into more than they can count or take credit for.

And that is the story of Jesus. Knowing who He was, He defied the notion of what Messiah "should be" by inviting twelve *unschooled, ordinary* men to follow and share life with Him. He intentionally invested Himself into them, modeling a lifestyle of intercession and intimacy with the Father, to which He then gave them access. Ultimately, Jesus entrusted the seeds of His life and the hope of His mission into the hands of men marked with imperfection, knowing that the seeds would grow and work to turn the world upside down.

Culture of the Few is not a discipleship model or a church planting method. It is the trust that the seeds of Christ still work. The culture of the few is the culture we find in the heart of Jesus to see the Father and see with the Father, and to do what we see the Father doing as we intentionally invest ourselves into those the Father gives us, inviting them into the place we have at His table.

If you want to change the world, follow after the ultimate Agent of Change. Rest in the fact that you belong to a Father who loves you because you belong to Him. Don't rush. Learn how to recognize what the Father is doing in the midst of the waiting and trust Him to lead you out of the carpenter's shop in His perfect timing.

Don't be afraid to love deeply and give yourself to ordinary people. Trust the Father to multiply the life of Jesus through your own imperfections.

Give yourself to the hidden lifestyle of intimacy and intercession. Take time to see the Father and see with the Father. Spending time in His presence won't cause you to miss out on anything worth having.

Find Jesus. Know Jesus. Focus on Jesus. Follow Jesus.

Acknowledgements

Thank you to the many friends and family who have been a part of shaping the journey of this book. Your faithful support and encouragement have allowed me to finish this project.

To Our Test Readers: Thank you for becoming a valuable part of our process. Your feedback gave me the conviction to see this project through.

To Josh & Lacey Sturm, Jim Baker, Jesse Pratt, Jasmine Tate, Erik Fish, Brian Orme: Thank you for your friendship and willingness to endorse this book. I'm humbled by your support.

To Jim Erb, Guy Glass, John Weisman, Everett Whiteside, and Floyd McClung: Thank you for your faithful friendship and pouring endlessly into my life. I am grateful to have spiritual fathers and big brothers to speak truth into my family and our church community. Your love has shown me Jesus and encouraged me to allow Him to be the standard for living, loving and leading.

I want to especially thank Floyd McClung. Your coaching at the completion of this project brought courage to my heart. Thank you for loving my family and for expressing value in this book. We pray that you get better and have a full recovery.

To the AOX Family: I am so thankful for the way God has brought us together. The journey over the past five years has been the most beautiful, messy experience that I have ever had in learning to be the church together. It is a joy to be a part of our holy experiment with you.

To the McKoys, Caters, Ayers and Peddes: Thank you for your faithful support and love. To Tom and Marian McKoy, thank you for raising me in a home where Jesus was most important. You are incredible parents, and I am humbled to be your little boy. To my wife, Adriane, thank you for every step of the journey. No one has pointed me to Jesus more often than you. You are truly a gift from the Father to me. To Abigail, thank you for loving me so well. Becoming your daddy was one of the best things that ever happened to me. I pray that you will pick up the baton and run farther with Jesus than I can imagine. I love you!

To the COTF Team: It's not that I couldn't have done it without you, but rather that I didn't get it done until God brought us all together. **Carl Catedral**, thank you for being the team at the beginning of this writing project. You let me know that it was important to share these stories. **Alexander Catedral**, thank you for dreaming with me and valuing this message. More than anything you have done, thank you for loving me through the journey. **David Wade**, thank you for being the world-changer that could talk me through this content and for editing this book while guarding my voice. **Mike Weber**, thank you for everything you have done and for sharing your stunning photography. You have added so much of Jesus to our team. **Michael Giffone**, thank you helping to create resources that will impact lives for Jesus. **Cody Weber**, thank you for investing your time to create and develop the next steps of *Culture of the Few*. **Katy Westra**, well beyond the beauty of your design work, you have truly embraced and helped shape the message of this book. Thank you. **Jessie Woodard**, Thank you for helping me develop this content by living it out with me for the last twelve years. Your work on the workbook has created a resource that will help many walk through important paradigm shifts. **Micah List**, thank you for bringing the handcrafted, original feel of your artwork to our cover. It is an honor to know you and follow Jesus together. **Stephanie McCloskey**, thank you for your patience and leadership in designing the cover of this book. It needed your touch! **Candise Wade**, God knew what He was doing when He brought you to our team. He has poured Himself into you in a way that is stunning. Thank you for helping me cross the finish line and for loving and supporting my heart. **Derek Kelly**, thank you for the way you have come alongside me. I know that you and Lora have sacrificed so much in the process. Words can't express my gratitude for the way you have loved me and my family and valued what God has put inside of our hearts. You are one of my heroes. Thank you.